Jon Udry is a juggler and stand-up comedian whose charming, frank and funny performances leave audiences on the edge of their seats and rolling in the aisles from laughter.

This winning combination has won him the award for 'British Young Juggler of the Year' and has led to appearances on radio and television, as well as appearing all over the world to international acclaim.

jonudry.com | @jonudry

THE ABC TOUR

A Juggler's Journey from A to Z

JON UDRY

MODERN VAUDEVILLE PRESS

PHILADELPHIA, PA

CONTENTS

FOREWORD

By Sam Veale

Jon first explained the concept of The ABC Tour during one of our regular *"business meetings"* at a trendy coffee shop in central London. He told me he was planning to do twenty-six shows at twenty-six venues, each venue beginning with a consecutive letter of the alphabet.

Initially, I was surprised that Jon knew what order the alphabet went in and I buried the urge to congratulate him on memorising the whole thing. I was about to suggest that he learnt some basic arithmetic as well, and perhaps some finger painting, when he continued.

There were rules to this tour, Jon explained. One of the most important was that each location had to be a non-venue where you would not expect to see a show. I cast a small shadow of doubt on this by explaining that the reason performers performed in performing venues, was that performing venues were designed for performers to perform in. Thankfully, Jon ignored this.

On a few occasions in my career, I have taken one look at a venue and decided the show was going to go badly long before it had even started. To me, The ABC Tour represented a perfect opportunity to do this twenty-six times in a row, but I realised that Jon was exactly the sort of energetic optimist that could pull it off.

We then had the first of many similar conversations, brainstorming venue ideas for each letter. This was always fun but Jon never used a single one of my suggestions. I don't have a problem with this but I still think that the letter 'X' should have been at an *'X-Girlfriend's House'*. The tour was supposed to be a challenge after all!

Jon Udry | ©*Beinn Muir*

PROLOGUE

I am a writer in the same way that someone assembling flat-pack furniture is a carpenter or that someone making beans on toast is a chef. That being said, here I am writing a book.

It's a book about the most difficult and testing project I've ever taken on, one that took me more than two years to complete and challenged me in ways that I never anticipated.

Allow me to tell you a little bit about myself. My name is Jon Udry and I am a juggler and comedian. I was born in Cornwall and now live in Bristol. At the time of writing this I am thirty-two years old and have been juggling for almost two and a half decades, since the tender age of six. I am lucky enough to regularly perform my comedy and juggling shows all over the world at festivals, corporate events, in cabarets and on cruise ships.

While the circumstances may vary hugely, these gigs all have some things in common. There is nearly always a stage, a lighting rig, a PA system and a microphone. The audience is typically seated and expecting to see a show. Over the years I have performed on many stages of this ilk and, not wanting to brag, I feel like I have the best job ever. I get to travel the world, visit interesting places, do what I love and get paid for the privilege of doing so. All of this makes me a very lucky guy.

I love that one week I can be on a cruise ship in the Caribbean, performing for 2,000 people in a packed-out theatre, and then the next week find myself in a damp, dimly-lit pub basement with my feet sticking to the floor while I perform for ten people.

It's incredibly humbling and, as much as I love to travel and perform for big audiences in idyllic venues, I honestly get more of a kick out of performing in challenging environments. During my career I've enjoyed doing shows in living rooms, bunkers, car parks and gardens. I loved taking locations where shows don't usually occur and transforming them into temporary theatres.

This is where The ABC Tour came in.

Many years ago, I saw one of my all-time favourite jugglers, Jay Gilligan, perform a show at a juggling festival in Paris called *Maison de Jonglage*. This particular show was set in what looked like a garage: it had low ceilings, no natural light and all of the surfaces were incredibly dusty. In short, it was idyllic for this particular show. Jay controlled the lights and sound by himself whilst doing a mind-blowing, hour-long performance. While I really enjoyed it, it got me thinking about what this venue was typically used for. Was it actually a garage? Who owned it? Did the owners know that they possessed such a brilliant, unconventional venue? How might I, as a performer, take non-venues such as this and temporarily transform them into the perfect space for a performance?

Over time, the concept for The ABC Tour came together. The plan was relatively simple – perform twenty-six shows, each taking place in a challenging venue starting with a different letter of the alphabet.

When this idea was brewing I was represented exclusively by a management company. They had promised to help me with my career and told me that, if I had any novel ideas, they would love to chat about them and support me in making them happen.

When I came to them with my initial pitch for The ABC Tour, they said it was a terrible idea that would be a complete waste of time and wouldn't make any money. Well, they were partly right. The ABC Tour was never a profit-making exercise – but that's not why I am in this business. There are easier ways to make money than spending over two decades trying to master the art of juggling, after all.

The initial plan was to do some crowdfunding through Kickstarter – an all-or-nothing crowdfunding platform – to raise money for the tour. To do this I met up with my friend, known professionally as "The Void", who helped me plan the tour and film a video for a Kickstarter campaign. Whilst we raised quite a lot of money through crowdfunding, we unfortunately missed out on our target. I was left disheartened and shelved my plans for The ABC Tour.

A few months passed and I found myself feeling ill just before I performed a show at a hotel in Rhodes, Greece. I managed to get through the show on adrenaline and then, after a quick snack, collapsed in bed out of exhaustion.

The next morning, I woke up in agony, with painful stabbing feelings in my stomach and lower back. I assumed it was a digestive issue that I attributed to the whole pack of post-show Pringles I'd demolished the night before. I was due to fly back to the UK later that day, but not until almost midnight. I battled through the day, despite the pain increasing in intensity to the point where I could barely walk.

I managed to make it to the nearest pharmacy and – after an embarrassing game of charades to cover for my complete lack of Greek – I bought some laxatives.

At this point, I was about to be picked up and taken to the airport, so it would've been a terrible time to administer the laxatives. At the airport, I had the same problem; the last thing I wanted was to be roaring it out on the toilet while my flight was boarding. I was now lying on the floor, barely able to move.

Jon Udry | ©Beinn Muir

To make matters worse, I had people who'd seen my show the night before coming up and telling me they'd enjoyed my performance.

When it came to boarding, I had no choice but to tell the air hostess that I was ill, which led to pandemonium as they decided whether or not I should be allowed to fly. Several calls to a doctor later, they agreed to let me board – although by this point the flight was seriously delayed. What the fifty or so people on the plane who'd seen my show thought at this point I don't know, but I doubt they were very sympathetic. It must have looked like I was suffering the after-effects of excessive drugs or booze from an after-show party. Little did they know, I was more of a Pringles party kind of guy.

Halfway through the flight I started to shake uncontrollably, like a leaf being tossed around by a hurricane. The air hostess wrapped me in a blanket and gave me some tea, which with shaking hands I managed to spill all over myself, leaving me with wet and scalded legs. I had no idea what was happening to me and I was more scared than I've ever been, before or since.

The air crew called ahead and an ambulance was waiting for me on the runway when we landed, which immediately sped off towards the nearest hospital. I was informed that I had appendicitis and the shaking was the result of my body going into toxic shock as my appendix burst into smithereens at 30,000 feet. It was the first time that I thought I might die – and I almost did.

People say that you only really start living after you almost die. This felt true for me: it was the wake-up call I needed to up my game and crack on. After a few well-needed months of recuperation from the surgery, I was back in shape and ready to get going with my career again. But first, I wanted to do something big. Something that would challenge me. Something unique, that no one had done before. Something that would be a physical, as well as a practical and mental challenge. I decided that I would go ahead with The ABC Tour, funding or not!

The concept of The ABC Tour was remarkably simple: a tour of twenty-six shows in twenty-six different venues, one for each letter of the alphabet. Before starting, I set myself strict rules as to the types of venues I would choose.

These rules made the process a lot trickier, but they also challenged me to perform in much more bizarre and tricky places – exactly what I was trying to do with the tour.

They were as follows:

NO PLACE NAMES

So I couldn't do
'A is for Australia' or
'B is for Bristol'

NO BRANDS

So that meant
'S is for Starbucks' and
'B is for Burger King'
were both out.

NO ADJECTIVES OF PLACES

What this means if that an
Italian Restaurant wouldn't be
'I is for Italian', it would be
'R is for Restaurant'.

NO OWNERSHIP

I could feasibly do
'G is for Garage', but I
wouldn't be able to perform
in Tim's Garage for 'T'.

While I was gutted not to have hit our crowdfunding target for The ABC Tour, this proved to be a blessing in disguise, as it meant that I could be 100% in charge of where (and when) I performed. If we had raised the money as originally planned, I would have been forced to perform in a variety of places that certain backers had suggested, as being able to choose a location was one of the rewards for supporting the Kickstarter campaign. By not having the pressure of any backers (or any funding!), I didn't need to jump through anyone else's hoops. After all, if I wasn't being paid by anyone, I could do whatever I wanted!

Armed with the realisation that this was a labour of love, I embraced the do-it-yourself mentality. At the time I thought this was the beginning of a six-month journey. Little did I know what I was in for…

---

*NB: When I started writing this book, I tried a couple of "hacks" to improve my limited vocabulary. My favourite – and by far the easiest – was downloading an app to my phone called 'Word of the Day'. As you can probably guess, this teaches you a new word each day. My favourite word so far is **Abecedarian** – a person who is just learning, a novice. This perfectly describes me in this current moment in time; after all, I am a novice at writing books. Then again, you've just bought a book by someone with limited writing skills. Bigger fool you!*

A IS FOR AQUARIUM

As I knew I'd have to get twenty-six different venues on board for the tour, the first show needed to be spectacular in order to set a precedent.

I started by writing a list of places beginning with 'A' and ranked them in order from best to worst. This list covered a wide range of both good and bad ideas, from an arena or an aviary to an arboretum and, possibly the worst idea of the lot, an abattoir. Right at the top of the list – outshining all of the other ideas – was to perform a show at an aquarium.

Armed with a list of the possible places that I might be able to persuade to get on board with the tour, I prepared myself for a long day working my way gradually down the list, crossing off the places that foolishly (or sensibly) didn't want me performing at their venue.

I flipping love a good aquarium, so I was excited at the idea of performing at one. At the same time, I didn't want to get my hopes up too high. I was fully expecting there to be a lot of red tape and all sorts of hoops to jump through in order to make this show – and all the future ABC Tour shows – happen. Taking a deep breath, I picked up the phone and dialled the number for Bristol Aquarium.

This was it. The process of getting the ABC Tour off the ground started right now.

Here is how I remember the conversation going:

Aquarium:
Hello, Bristol Aquarium

Me:
Hello. My name is Jon Udry and I am a juggler and a comedian. I have a slightly unusual request, but is there somebody that I could talk to about running a possible event, please?

Aquarium:
That would be me. I'm Hannah, the manager. How can I help?

Me:
Great! Well, I have this idea called The ABC Tour. It is a tour of 26 different venues, one for each letter of the alphabet. Now as you are aware, A is the first letter of the alphabet.

Aquarium:
Yes, I am aware of this.

Me:
Would there be any chance that I might be able to do a show at your Aquarium?

Aquarium:
Well, actually... yes!

It turned out that the Aquarium staff were having an event in a few weeks time and they were planning on going bowling. Hannah thought that, as a surprise for the rest of the employees, they could watch my show once the aquarium closed for the day, before hitting the lanes.

In my head, I was anticipating getting to the fourth or fifth option on my list before anyone even considered saying yes to this ludicrous idea.

But here I was: first idea, first phone call, 100% success rate. Hook, line and sinker. Given this early success, I naively thought the rest of The ABC Tour was going to be a breeze.

Even though I couldn't invite the general public to this event, I still wanted to make a poster advertising that I was going to do the show and that the tour had started. I really loved the idea that at the end of the tour, I'd have twenty-six different posters for the shows that I'd done, almost like a medal of achievement.

Like writing, I had no experience with creating or designing a poster, but thought I'd give it a good try. I had never used Adobe Photoshop before and was dumbfounded by the labyrinth of riddles, puzzles and mazes I had to navigate in order to create anything that even resembled an image on the screen.

Its complexities were way above my head, and it took me almost four hours of stressing, swearing and sweating to create a poster that, quite frankly, was pretty rubbish. However, it would have to do for now as I only had one laptop, and another hour of wrestling with the Photoshop algorithms would surely force me to throw it out of the window. I couldn't take that risk.

On the day of the gig, I was joined by my good friend Sam Veale. I mean, he'd have to be a good friend to drive for two hours to help out with a weird project in an aquarium for no money. But that's what friends are for, I told him.

One of the plans for The ABC Tour was to turn it into a mini web-series and later, a documentary. So as well as moral and technical support, it was Sam's job to film the performance.

Before arriving at the gig, I was very anxious about the way the show would look through the lens of the camera. This remained a constant worry of mine throughout The ABC Tour. The last thing I wanted was for the gig to take place in some anonymous conference room, or events room where they hold kids' birthday parties. If I was going to be performing at an aquarium, I needed it to look like an aquarium.

We arrived a few hours early so that Hannah could give us a tour and show us a few options for performance locations. It also gave us the opportunity to take a look at the fish whilst Hannah gave us a mini guided tour.

One creature I was particularly interested to see was an electric eel called Bolt. Hannah told us that he had been confiscated at customs at a London airport from someone that was trying to smuggle him into the country from the Amazon Rainforest.

I pondered the logistics of electric eel smuggling and decided that organising The ABC Tour, however complicated, was probably simpler.

Following our mini guided tour, we were stunned to be given permission to perform in the very place where we wanted the show to happen – right in front of the main fish tank. No hoops to jump through. No red tape. I was going to perform with fish as the backdrop, swimming about like a desktop screensaver. Perfect.

As soon as the last of the public had left for the day, Sam and I got to

work with getting the show ready. I was set to do a 30-minute show that would culminate in my helium balloon juggling routine. I wanted to finish with this as I thought the effect of the floating objects would look fantastic against the background of hundreds of floating fish. Well, hopefully not "floating" fish, but you know what I mean[1].

Sam came up with a bright idea: instead of the plain white helium balloons that I normally use, I could use topical balloons from the aquarium gift shop – a shark, a mermaid and some fish. Remarkably,

Photo: Sam Veale

[1] With such a big tank containing so many fish, I couldn't help but wonder what they did with the inevitable occasional dead one. I like to think that they have a massive toilet in the back room that they flush them down. I didn't want to ask. I feel that the mystery is probably more appealing than the truth.

we were allowed to do this as well. Anarchy.

After getting changed in the store cupboard, we set up the "stage". Throughout my years in the industry, I have often had to get changed in small pokey places – and this store cupboard was no exception. It had the classics: an obligatory mop, a stack of chairs, some kind of boiler and just enough room for one person to stand. After getting ready and stepping out into the "venue", it was surprising to see how something as simple as a couple of industrial lights from a hardware store, a microphone stand, some benches and an amplifier could transform this tranquil aquarium into a temporary theatre.

Once the set-up was complete, I sat on the bench where the audience would be sitting in a few moments time and watched the fish swimming around. It was a paradoxical situation; I have never felt so stressed whilst looking at something so peaceful in my entire life. It was a bit like having a relaxing massage while knowing that you've left the oven on.

The audience arrived and it was time to actually begin the tour. The first steps into a journey of unknown length. The show was a complete surprise to the staff, apart from Hannah, and it went down a storm.

As enjoyable as it was to be performing my classic bits of material in front of the aquarium, the highlight for me was the helium balloon routine. Juggling with helium balloons is problematic

at the best of times due to drafts, inconsistencies of float-ability and weight, but this time I had the added variable of the balloons all being different sizes too. This made it extra fun for me as I had to adapt the routine as I went along by figuring out whether the balloon fish would float a little quicker than the balloon shark, and the balloon mermaid was surprisingly the quickest floater of them all (that sentence probably hasn't been written before).

As I was performing, I wondered what the thousands of fish were thinking about the chaos going on outside of their tank. As there were a hundred times more fish than humans at my show, you could argue that it was partly for them as well.

In an ideal world, I would have put a waterproof camera in the tank and filmed the show from the fishes' point of view, perhaps with a fisheye lens, but this was rightfully prohibited as it could be bad for the fish.

Performing at Bristol Aquarium was truly an honour and a great way to kick off The ABC Tour. Having the opportunity to start the tour there, in front of such a lovely crowd of humans (and fish), made me feel extremely fortunate.

B IS FOR BAKERY

B ristol has an abundance of delightful coffee shops. Immediately after booking *A is for Aquarium* I rewarded myself with a coffee from my favourite local, The Bristol Loaf.

The Bristol Loaf is a trendy, artisan coffee shop and bakery. Their bread and croissants are the best I've ever had. At the time of writing, The Bristol Loaf has doubled in size and delivers their wonderful baked goods all over the city to various independent companies. However, back at the beginning of the tour, the bakery and coffee shop was fairly small and very cosy. While there, I happened to bump into the owners, Gary and Alex, and we got chatting about how our respective days had gone. Still riding the wave of enthusiasm, I had a sudden epiphany. Bakery began with a 'B'!

Me:
Hey! Do you think we could do a show here?

Gary:
If you think there's enough room in here, then yes!

Done! Two in one day – as if it was meant to be. Ignoring the fact that there really was barely enough room, we quickly worked out a convenient date and

B is for Bakery was born. We chose the day after *A is for Aquarium* for the performance, with the notion that I could start lining up future ABC Tour gigs in the days that followed. In a spate of incredibly misguided optimism, I was starting to believe that we'd have this whole thing wrapped up within a couple of months.

At this stage, I had been impressed by how The ABC Tour was being greeted with such warmth at every turn. So far, everyone I had asked was eager to give it a chance and had proven both welcoming and keen to help. Both Hannah and Gary were 'Yes' people – I really love 'Yes' people. For this show, Gary had even offered to keep his coffee shop open after hours, so that he could serve food and drink to the anticipated audience members that would flock to the show.

I had my concerns about this show as it was the first one on the tour that would be open to the public. *A is for Aquarium* was a private event with a guaranteed audience but *B is for Bakery* had no such guarantee and I became convinced that nobody would turn up.

This time I needed all the publicity I could get, which meant slogging my way through Photoshop's quagmire once more in order to squeeze out another sub-par poster. Luckily, my friend Anton Mackman stepped in to help. When I say "help," I mean that he made a new poster all by himself. It looked great and, just to make me feel even worse, it only took him twenty minutes. For the rest of the tour, Anton was the go-to poster guy.

On the day of the performance, I was joined once again by my friend Sam. I was incredibly anxious about this show for a number of reasons. Firstly, there was very little space for me to perform in. Normally when I perform, I require an area of at least 3 metres squared. For *B is for Bakery*, my "stage" was roughly one square metre. I could barely move. If I had a cat swinging routine, I'd have to cut it out of the show.

Not only was the space tiny but I was also surrounded by breakable items. To my right was a window; to my left, a glass cabinet displaying their fine pastry goods and above me were some delicate hanging lights. It was the juggling equivalent of threading a rope through the eye of a needle, except the rope was made of toothpaste, and the eye of the needle was closed.

Secondly, as people were coming out specifically to see the show, I felt that I had to prepare more material to make it worth their while. I set myself the challenge of doing an hour but, as I wasn't actually sure if anyone would turn up, I decided not to include any audience participation just in case there wasn't

Photos: Sam Veale

enough of an audience to participate. It would be an hour all by myself, which was daunting as hell.

Thirdly, I really love The Bristol Loaf. If the show didn't go well then I would never be able to show my face there again. There was a lot at stake.

Stood between an industrial oven and a large mixer, I changed into my three piece suit. In spite of my pessimism, an audience started to trickle in. For the show itself, I would be sandwiched between the audience and the bakery's shop window. There was nobody to announce the start of the show so I took the microphone out onto the street and introduced myself, while looking at the audience through the window. For me, this absurd image was a particularly fun way to start the show and I think it gave the audience a taste of what was to come.

During the show I loved that people from the street could look in and – unlike the fish at *A is for Aquarium* – they could interact with the performance from the other side of the glass. On a number of occasions people tapped on the glass or tooted their car horns. This opened up plenty of opportunities for improvisation, which I always welcome.

At one point, a drunk man walked in, brown paper bag in hand, to see what on earth was going on. After an attempted conversation he left the bakery looking somewhat confused. I like to think that when he sobered up, the vague memory of a comedy juggling show in a bakery would make him think that maybe he'd had one brown bag too many and that this cured him of his alcoholism. We'll never know.

This show turned out to be more of a success than I'd anticipated. Not only did people actually turn up, but the show went down well. I had a great time performing in the bakery and it made me question why I don't do it more often!

My plan for The ABC Tour was that I'd try and perform something unique at each show that would contextually make sense in that specific setting (such as the fish balloons in the *A is for Aquarium*). Gary had even put aside some old baguettes that I was planning on using for a routine. However, I only realised that I'd forgotten to do so about three hours after the show had finished, and to be honest, it was a bit late at that point.

This show taught me to pay more attention to making venue-specific routines. It would've been nice to have a minute of unique material from each show so that, at the end, I could compile them into a 26-minute ABC

Tour Show. Unfortunately I missed my chance of doing this on only the second performance!

When *B is for Bakery* was over, Sam said, "Once the show begins, it's easy to forget that you are in a bakery or an aquarium". I love that, with just a seating arrangement and a few simple lights, you can temporarily transform regular spaces into theatres. I also like to think that one day somebody will come back to the bakery and – just for a couple of seconds – they might think, *Wasn't there a juggling show in here?*

Two years after this gig, I watched a stand-up special on Netflix by comedy genius Maria Bamford called *Old Baby*. In this special, Bamford performs her quirky stand-up show in a variety of locations such as her living room, to people sitting on a park bench and in a library. One of the locations that I was particularly envious of was a bowling alley. In hindsight, I think this would've been a better setting for 'B' on The ABC Tour, but, just like remembering about the baguette trick, this came to me all too late.

When I set out on The ABC Tour, my aim was to efficiently book the gigs and get them ticked off the list. So much so that I wasn't really that fussed about where they were. I went to The Bristol Loaf, saw a booking opportunity and acted on impulse to get the performance set in scone. *B is for Bakery* was a lot of fun and it went well but I feel like the better gigs on The ABC Tour were still to come, when I had to overcome some real logistical challenges. But I'll baguette to those later (no bun intended).

C IS FOR CASTLE

Considering my first attempt at getting The ABC Tour off the ground didn't work out, it wasn't a complete failure. In fact, the publicity from it actually helped when it came to tackling the tour the second time around. One of my backers on the Kickstarter campaign was Tom Humphreys, who pledged a generous sum for me to perform at a venue of his choice.

As we didn't reach our crowdfunding target, his pledge had been cancelled but, as The ABC Tour was back on its feet, I decided to get in touch with Tom to see if he was still interested in being involved.

Tom's family owns a delightful castle in Usk, South Wales, and he jumped at the chance to host an ABC Tour performance there.

Coincidentally, Tom was getting married soon, so we decided to combine his bachelor party with *C is for Castle*. This came with two benefits. Firstly, I'd have a guaranteed crowd and secondly, he'd have a free show as part of his stag do. Again, I was struck by how easy it was to arrange these shows and I was convinced that the rest of the tour would be a breeze. My delusions were very much real at this point.

For this particular gig, I reluctantly decided to perform fire juggling as it fit with the medieval setting. Personally, I hate fire juggling. I hate that when someone first discovers that I am a juggler, one of the first things they ask is, "Do you juggle fire?". In my opinion, it is a vastly overrated skill, it's dirty and it makes your clothes smell bad. I hate it!

The fact that people still juggle fire seems awfully dated to me. I loathe the faux "danger" element that comes with it. I hate all danger juggling[2] (with chainsaws and knives and whatnot) for the same reason.

I understand that from the audience's perspective it looks dangerous. *The fire torches could set the performer on fire! The chainsaw could cut them in half! The knives could chop their arms off!* But this is never going to happen. Why would it? Why would someone who works with their hands put themselves in actual danger for a room of people that they don't know for a bit of money? With the amount of people that perform "danger juggling", if it were truly dangerous, surely we would see more jugglers with fingers missing, burn wounds and fewer limbs.

Nobody who is level-headed would do that. The danger is not real. There is no risk. When you light a fire torch, it doesn't have a lot of time to heat up. The flame is going upwards, so the worst-case scenario is that you catch it on the wrong end and you simply just drop it. This is the absolute worst-case scenario. Well, unless you are performing at a petrol station, in which case, if you're juggling with fire then you deserve the sizzling end that comes to you.

With chainsaws, the engine is running but the blades have been dulled down or replaced with a bicycle chain – so you'd struggle to even cut through a small hedge. As for the knives: clearly, these are not real knives. Jugglers tend to travel a lot for work and we get our bags checked regularly at airports, just like everyone else. Do you really think that airport security isn't going to get a little bit suspicious when they notice three razor-sharp machetes in your baggage? Of course they are.

So that's why I hate fire. It's fake and insincere. Okay, rant over.

---

[2] *I don't hate all danger juggling: there is one exception. I am a huge fan of the American magicians, Penn and Teller. Penn Jillette has a fantastic juggling section in their show. I am not sure if it is fake and I really do not want to know as it may alter how I feel about it. Jillette takes three liquor bottles and, holding them by the neck, smashes the base of the bottles off. He is now holding three jagged, unevenly weighted, seemingly genuinely dangerous objects. He then juggles them. Beautiful.*

Prior to this gig, I hadn't juggled
fire for seven years. After
rummaging through my props, I
dug out and dusted off my old fire
clubs and found I had one less than
I thought. I really wanted to finish
by juggling five, but I only had four. I
called my reliable pal (and East Bristol's top
children's entertainer) Marky Jay to borrow an
additional fire club. After a ropey practice session
in his back garden, I felt ready.

My friend Sam, who had been there to help me with the
first two shows, was now unavailable. So was the next person I asked
– and the next. My anxiety and paranoia kicked in and convinced me that
everyone I knew was having a big, anti-ABC Tour party and I hadn't even been
invited.

In hindsight, that probably didn't happen, but it still left me with no one
to film, take photos or help out. Rescheduling *C is for Castle* for another date
was out of the question so I prepared myself for a few hours of multitasking.
Jugglers are supposed to be good at that after all.

On the day of the show, I met Tom and the rest of the Humphreys family at the
castle and wandered the grounds, scouting out ideal performing locations. Tom
recommended that we use the original gateway to the castle, which was decorated
with all the medieval ornamentation you might expect: taxidermy, killing-holes
and a rather large cannon. Someone had even set up some stage lights as well,
which was great because it was one less thing that I had to worry about.

This location really did look beautiful. The lights bounced around the
medieval brickwork of the castle's gateway, framing it much like the proscenium
of a theatre. Later I learnt that the gateway to the castle was where enemies
would typically try and break in – at which point the gates would close,
trapping the baddies within the small space between the castle and the doors.
Once the scoundrels had nowhere to escape, the guards would drop hot oil
through the killing-holes in the ceiling onto the enemies, to serve them bloody
right for trying to break in in the first place. But tonight, it was being used for
juggling and comedy.

I questioned Tom about the stage lights and he introduced me to a friend
of the family, Steve. He just so happened to be staying at the Humphreys'
residence for a few days and had set up the lights which he'd had in his car
from a professional videography gig he'd just finished. That's right. Steve was a
cameraman. He was exactly what I needed and didn't have.

After an attempt at slinging some charm his way, Steve agreed to film the show. So now I didn't have to worry about lights – or a camera! I was half expecting Tom to introduce me to a friend that could offer to do my show for me as well. I couldn't really get any luckier, could I? Couldn't I?

It turns out that yes, I could. Tom then introduced me to a couple of friends who were in a band together, called the Happy Child Tour. The Happy Child Tour were – as their name suggested – on a tour themselves, and happened to be passing through Usk on the way to perform another gig the following day. Coincidentally, they had offered to perform at Tom's stag do on the same night as *C is for Castle*. Not only were they happy for me to use their amplification system and microphone (another thing I now didn't have to worry about!) but they were also very keen on some sort of collaboration with me. Yahtzee!

The evening's running order ended up going as follows; I would perform an hour-long comedy and juggling show, they would come on stage to join me for the finale, and then I would leave the stage for them to carry on with the rest of their set.

We decided that it would be best for me to finish by fire juggling with the band, because then it meant they could play a song whilst I went and got changed into something that I didn't mind getting covered in stinky, hot paraffin splashback. Then I would rejoin them on stage and finish the show in true medieval fashion with some fire juggling to accompany their second song.

With the schedule sorted and logistics in the bag, a lot of the weight had been lifted from my shoulders. Now all we needed was an audience. *C is for Castle* was the first ABC Tour show that I'd performed outside of Bristol, which gave me a whole new barrel of concerns. As mentioned before, we did have a small group of people who were there to attend Tom's stag do but, to be honest, I would've felt pretty awful if we had gone through the effort of hiring out a castle, setting up the lights, camera and band, if the only people who actually saw it were the stag do attendees (Stag Doers? Staggerers? Maybe by the end of the evening).

Fortunately, this was not the case. As the evening drew closer, excited people started to turn up at the castle, asking if this is where the juggling show was taking place.

Just take that in for a moment. What a wonderfully bizarre thing to have to ask. Is the juggling and comedy show at this castle? As opposed to the other castle down the road? Lovely stuff.

As if my nerves weren't rattling enough, I began to notice a couple of familiar faces in the crowd. My relatives had descended upon The ABC Tour, namely my Uncle, my Auntie, my Dad's cousin, and even my Great Uncle Alec, who was 92. It was so nice to see them and for them to come and support my show – but I also find it very difficult to perform in front of people I know, especially family. The pressure ramped up.

Despite my concerns, and the castle's dog running through the stage at various and precarious moments, the show went like clockwork. The crowd lapped up the fire juggling, and with the support from the Happy Child Tour and the sun setting at just the right moment, it created quite a magical atmosphere. This is one of the reasons I love my job, and in particular, this tour. A moment was created in a live show, that only a select few people got to see – and this will never be repeated the same way again. Sure, people will be able to see it in the video, but it's never quite the same as experiencing it live.

That being said, I still hate fire juggling.

After the show, I managed to hang out with my family for a bit. My Great Uncle Alec played the 'Classic Uncle' card and offered to give me some money. I declined. He insisted. I took the money. I'm no fool. This was, and still is at the time of writing, the most amount of money I earned from The ABC Tour.

It was £20.

D IS FOR DOOR SHOP

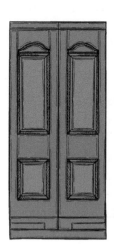

Despite having twenty-three shows left to book and perform on the tour, I was filled with nothing but joy, enthusiasm and optimism. With the tyres still warm on The ABC Tour Bus following the success of 'A', 'B' and 'C', I assumed it would be plain sailing from here on out. Then 'D' happened.

For the first time, I was utterly stumped. My first idea was a dungeon. I liked the idea of being in some kind of cage (maybe that says more about me than you really need to know!). The downside was that it would be very similar to the idea I already had in mind for 'J': jail. I contacted the only dungeons that I could find and they were not keen on the idea at all which, to be honest, was probably a good thing, as I was in a relationship at the time.

After this first set of rejections, I had to go to my second idea for 'D': Dog Shelter. I thought it would be a great idea to get some footage of me attempting to do a juggling show for dogs, along with some specifically written dog-based comedy. I contacted a dog shelter and pitched the idea to them by saying that I would make a fun video, and would, in turn, advertise their shelter and chosen charity. How could you say no to that? Don't ask me, ask them. Also ask the seven other dog shelters that I contacted. I don't know why, but every single dog damn one of them said no. In hindsight, again, it was probably a good thing. It would have made a funny video, but would it have qualified as a show? I'm not so sure.

Having hit a significant hurdle, the momentum of The ABC Tour subsided for a few weeks. I spent this time doing what I would normally do; juggling, gigging and drinking coffee. I had started to get a bit fed up that I couldn't think of anything good for 'D', it also played on my mind that this was delaying the organisation of the other twenty-two venues that I still had to come up with and get booked in. As I was trying to do the shows in alphabetical order, I couldn't book any of the rest of the tour until 'D' was set in stone.

I frustratedly started to write down a list of words beginning with 'D'; dentist, door, dog, diving board, drive, doctors etc… (you know what words beginning with 'D' look like, I didn't have to do that). Then I went through this list and jotted down my issues with each:

DENTIST

I hate the dentist and, if I was in the dentist, the last thing I'd want to see is a comedy juggling act.

DOG SHELTER

They didn't want me. If only they knew what it felt like to be unwanted and rejected.

DOCTOR'S SURGERY

Same problem as the Dentist

DOOR

It's a noun, not a place.

DRIVING

Way too dangerous.

DIVING BOARD

Not a bad idea but I really, really hate heights.

On my way home from guzzling an oat milk flat white from The Bristol Loaf, I had a eureka moment. I drove past a shop called Door World. I quickly turned the car around (obeying all of the rules of the road – I'm not a barbarian) and parked up outside to pay them a visit. As I walked in I was greeted by a very friendly man who worked there, Gary Shrimpton, and my anxiety immediately melted away. While I couldn't do a show on or in a door, I could definitely perform a show in a door shop, *surrounded* by doors.

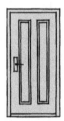

From Gary's friendly tone, I had a very strong feeling that he'd be on board, so I hit him with the usual spiel. As I explained, he smiled and nodded along. I became conscious of the fact that I was smiling and nodding along with him. I stopped, worried he would think I was mocking him. Luckily he didn't seem to notice.

It turned out that Gary was very keen, and we set a date for *D is for Door Shop* there and then. Trying my best to ignore the fact that I had just broken my first rule of the

tour by this technically being *S is for Shop*, I was thrilled to have found a venue.

Not only was I relieved to have something filling the D-shaped hole in The ABC Tour, but this was the moment where I gained a lot more faith in this ridiculous project. Who on earth would let a juggler do a show in their door shop? Gary, that's who. We all need to be a little bit more like Gary.

The day of the show soon whipped around and, as usual, I convinced myself that no one would turn up.

It was a recurring theme during The ABC Tour that I worried there would be at least one show where there would be no audience. This time around, however, I had good reason to be concerned.

It was twenty minutes until showtime and there was no one in sight. My mind raced, trying to work out what I should do if there was no audience. Should I go ahead with it anyway? If I didn't do the show, surely that would mean I hadn't done 'D', so I'd have to either perform to no one, or find and set up another 'D' show, hoping that people would come to it, and I'd

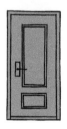

already exhausted my 'D-list' options.

At this point it seemed like there was a common factor about the people that came to my shows; they liked turning up at the last minute. I'm convinced this is entirely due to the fact that they think that I thrive off nerves and anxiety. Maybe they think that they'll get a better show if I'm a stressed out mess.

The stage was framed nicely with a backdrop of doors from around the shop. Ideally, I had wanted to start the show by coming through a door in the back centre of the stage but, bizarrely, there were no doors on hinges in Door World. For that I suppose I'd have to have visited Hinge World (well, at least that's 'H' sorted!).

Instead, I created a passageway in the centre of the backdrop, made up of doors, that I would use to enter the stage. As it turns out, a corridor consisting entirely of doors (a corri-door) works surprisingly well.

I tried to create a new piece for this show using

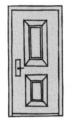

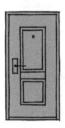
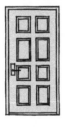
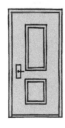

an incredibly inconvenient prop called poppers. Poppers are hemispheres that you turn inside out and leave on a flat surface. After an indeterminate amount of time, they will pop up into the air. Imagine a smooth tennis ball that has been sliced in half, turned inside out, and then suddenly snapping back into shape.

I would lay a number of poppers out on the floor, on parts of my body and on doors laid at various angles, and they would pop up into a juggling pattern. In theory, a good idea.

However, one of the many problems with poppers is that the time it takes for each popper to pop can be very different. One can purchase a plentiful pack of poppers from a popular proper popper pop-up shop (presumably Peter Piper is the proprietor) and, while they all look the same, they will all pop up after very different amounts of time. Preposterous.

An additional complication is that the amount that you pop a popper has a huge effect on the time it takes for them to pop. If you chuck in the fact that the room temperature plays an annoyingly large factor in the equation, then the entire routine becomes a nightmare to perform.

It was tense, which in my opinion is part of its winning charm, but I can honestly say that that particular routine didn't go well. I do still think there is something good to be made with poppers; however, I just haven't found it yet. People do say that poppers liven up any party. I guess I am not going to the right parties because my experience with them so far has been nothing but hellish.

After the show, as the giddy audience exited the venue with smiles on their faces, I was filled with a familiar post-show buzz.

Despite feeling good about the event, a part of me was also feeling a bit guilty. It was enjoyable and an honour to be performing in such a lovely door shop, but it was no challenge. Essentially, I did my show in a normal room, the only difference being the number of doors that it contained.

I felt like I had found a loophole in my own

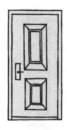

challenge of The ABC Tour, and I didn't feel great about it. A regular show in a regular room wasn't the purpose of The ABC Tour. I was so caught up in the single minded effort of keeping this tour on track, that I just wanted to get 'D' out of the way so that I could keep going.

Perhaps I should've tried to call a few more dog shelters. Either way, it was a great experience, and an important lesson on the tour was learned: don't take the path of least resistance.

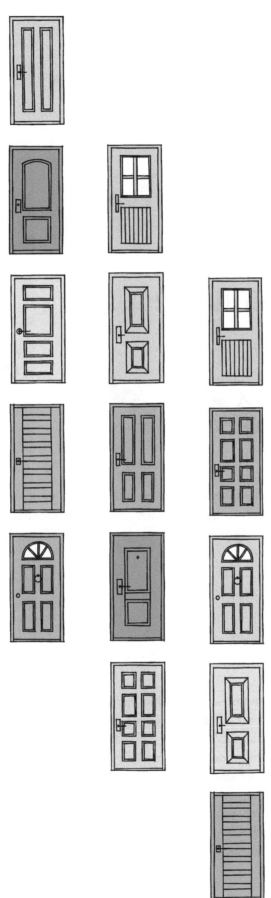

E IS FOR EDEN PROJECT

Eventually, with a tour like this, I knew I had to mess up somewhere along the line. My hands are up. I know. You got me. I know what you are thinking and I completely agree with you. I can practically hear you asking one of either two questions:

What is the Eden Project?

or

Surely doing a show at the Eden Project breaks one of your rules, right?

In response to those questions, I say, "Shut up. Just shut up!". It's really difficult to think of anything for 'E'. Plus, it's my tour, my rules.

In my defence, I could not for the life of me think of anything for 'E', so I contacted the Eden Project on a whim and they were very keen. Not a good excuse for rule breaking I know, but it's really all that I've got.

I spent weeks desperately trying to think of a possible venue for 'E'. I asked around. I brainstormed with people, but there was just no gold. I was aha!-less. My brain was *E was for Empty.*

Here are some of the ideas I came up with, so you can see why it was so tricky:

EEL FARM

You could argue that this is 'F is for Farm'. I also don't think it would look good on camera. And eels. Yuck!

ESCALATOR

Novel and whimsical, but of no real interest to me.

ELEVATOR

I only realised this after 'E', but part of the inspiration for the ABC Tour might have been a show in an elevator. In the comedy series 'Flight of

the Conchords', the musical duo's manager gets them several awful gigs, including one in an elevator. However, when performing in an elevator, it just looks like a small room – so that wouldn't work for the ABC Tour.

EMERGENCY ROOM

See Doctor and Dentist (Chapter D). Also, it's 'R is for Room'

END OF THE ROAD

Really clutching at straws, here.

To this day, I cannot think of a good option for 'E' on The ABC Tour, but no doubt as you are reading this, you'll think of one and feel the need to get in touch. I mean no disrespect, but please don't. I have long finished the tour and have even written a book about it. This knowledge will be of no use to me now.

One of the purposes for having the rules around venue selection was to ensure that all the shows took place in universally recognisable locations. Anyone in the world should be able to see one of the shows online, and instantly know what and where it was. The majority of the world knows what an aquarium, bakery or castle looks like but there is a very high chance that they don't know what (or where) the Eden Project is. This means that, because I have broken my own rules, I now have to provide an explanation.

The Eden Project is a popular tourist attraction in Cornwall. It consists of two large biomes containing plants collected from many diverse climates and environments. Each enclosure emulates a natural biome that consists of hundreds of hexagonal and pentagonal, inflated, plastic cells supported by steel frames. Basically, two extremely large greenhouses. The largest of the two biomes simulates a rainforest environment and the second, a Mediterranean environment. It's fantastic. If you ever get the chance to visit, you really should.

In booking the gig at the Eden Project, the staff were extremely helpful and really got the gist of what The ABC Tour was all about. Initially, they offered me a slot on a day when they already had lots of entertainment planned, so a lot of people were expected to attend and there would be stages set up with lights and sound. After explaining that I didn't really want to do a show on a stage as it wasn't really on brand with the tour, they suggested that I could do a show in the rainforest biome, as long as I didn't mind the humidity and the ants. Perfect. Now they were talking The ABC Tour language!

Walking into the rainforest biome to set up my equipment for the show, I was hit once more with just how absurd this tour was, and how lucky I was to do such an odd project. I was thinking to myself, *I just called them up. I asked to do a show. Now I am about to do a show in this insane venue.* I know this was the plan, but I hadn't actually expected them to say yes!

The first thing you notice when entering the rainforest biome is the humidity. I was wearing my classic showman attire, a three-piece suit, which instantly started to cling to my already sweaty body. What's more, from the very moment I placed my props down, I noticed the ants investigating my equipment. They inquisitively ambled over the juggling clubs, diabolos, balls and rings.

I wondered what they were thinking. From the way they were scurrying, it looked like they were excited for the show. I noticed they were very attracted to the microphone lead. Probably because of science or something.

The audience soon gathered, primed and ready for business. With approximately 200 people watching, this was the biggest audience on The ABC Tour so far.

About 20 of those attending were family members: Mum, Dad, Brothers, Sister, In-laws, Uncles, Aunties, Cousins, Nieces, Nephews, the lot. As I mentioned before, I always find it terrifying performing in front of my family. I hate it, and I'm not 100% sure why, either. Maybe I'm doing whatever I can to prevent that awkward conversation over Christmas dinner about how I should consider getting a "proper" career? Despite bracing myself for it, this conversation never actually happens because they have always been very supportive, especially my parents, so I know that the fear comes from deep within the depths of my insecurities.

Perhaps it was the fact that I am the only one in my family to venture into show business? Maybe I feel extra pressure because I really don't want to let them down? Maybe I was just crazy and covered in ants?

Before the show started, I was already as sweaty as I would normally be after a show that wasn't taking place in a rainforest biome. As the show went on, I became steadily more drenched. This wasn't helped by the fact that, every time I picked up the microphone or any of my props, I had to violently shake off a clump of creepy crawlies, which just made the sweating all the worse.

Luckily, I had anticipated the heat, so I'd planned to do my water juggling. This is essentially a routine where I pour water into plastic pint glasses and proceed to juggle, spill, twirl and fling the water around in a very loose attempt at not spilling any, whilst progressively creating more and more mess. It's chaos.

Performing this routine in the heat was absolute bliss and the audience didn't seem to mind a light splashing from the water either. At one point, a kid stood up from the crowd and walked into the performance space. As I was juggling two balls in one hand and holding a cup full of water in the other, I threw one ball high into the air and chucked the water over the kid's head. This got a mixed reaction; some cheered but others were concerned. The kid was my nephew, Harvey, but the audience didn't know that. As far as they were concerned, I had just waterboarded a random four-year-old. Now that's entertainment[3].

---

[3] No four-year-olds were injured during this show and – to this day – Harvey still receives a Christmas card from me every other year.

Photo: Pippa Moss

During this routine, I normally refill the cups with a larger jug that I have set aside, but for this particular gig, I thought it would be nice if I used a watering can. Unfortunately, the watering can that the Eden Project supplied for me was huge: I could barely lift it when it was full. This meant that when I poured into the cups, the trajectory of the water always fired WAY further than I expected.

Instead of the water landing in my cups as planned, it ended up filling a pram which, luckily, was empty. Apologies to the pram owners, who probably thought after the show that they needed to buy a new brand of nappies for their child. It wasn't your child that wet the pram, it was me[4].

E is for Eden Project really was a lot of fun and the audience was fantastic. There is a part of me that feels like I cheated the system too early and should have found an alternative for 'E' that fit more closely with the rules. If I ever do The ABC Tour again, and that's a big "if", I'll do my best to stick to my own rules a little more closely. Maybe.

---

[4] *I found out much later that the pram belonged to my niece, who receives the same prestigious Christmas card treatment as Harvey.*

F IS FOR FOREST

Frustratingly, The ABC Tour inspired many ideas that I wish I'd had much earlier. One of these better-late-than-never ideas happened when I reached 'F'.

There were a few possible venues for 'F', but nothing had been 100% confirmed. On another note, I was also struggling to gain traction with followers on social media. As an experiment, I decided to post the following across my various social media platforms:

"Ok, I am looking for suggestions for F on The ABC Tour. It needs to be a TYPE of place, not a place name. For example, Farm and Ferry are good. But France, Fred's house, Frome and Frank and Benny's are not good. Any suggestions?"

I was amazed with the response that I received. Within minutes, comments and suggestions were flooding in from friends, family, fans and foes (ok, not foes but I wanted another word beginning with 'F'). Even better, some of the suggestions were really quite good:

FARM

A nice idea but I already knew that I wanted to do 'Z is for Zoo' and this might be too similar.

FOUNTAIN

I really liked this and, to be honest, wish I'd chosen it. In my head I was going to do a water-based show later on in the Tour, so I passed on this.

FERRY

I've done shows on ferries in the past and the performance space looks like a standard theatre, so this was a no-go.

FIRE STATION

A solid contender. I liked the idea of doing a show for firefighters inside a station. Plus, I reckon they'd have let me have a whirl on the pole. Weeehey!

A friend of mine suggested a forest and I was instantly hooked on the idea. I loved how different it would look to the shows that I'd done so far. Another friend, Jennifer Davis, replied to the comment, saying that she had a forest that I could use as, at the time, she ran a forest school called Stonebury Learning, where the children learned whatever they wanted, whenever they were ready to learn. As the teacher, Jennifer's role was to guide them through various forest activities, such as making fires and building dens.

After chatting through logistics with Jennifer, we arranged a site visit to check out the lay of the land and before I knew it, the date was set for F is for Forest.

As there was no access to electricity where I wanted to perform, Jennifer came up with some great ideas about how we could illuminate the forest and make it look presentable. I would perform the show next to a big campfire and Jennifer would hang some beautiful candles in empty jars from the trees as decoration.

Once it was all set up, it looked marvellous. As the "venue" was lit by fire, I felt it was appropriate to perform fire juggling for the second (and hopefully last) time on The ABC Tour – and you know how I feel about that.

I feel this would be a good time to mention how I first started fire juggling. When I was nine years old, my parents would take me to local circus skills workshops, run by a lovely woman called Blossom the Clown. I love Blossom. She taught me all sorts of tricks with plate spinning, devilstick, club passing, diabolo etc.

It got to the point where I was keen to learn more and there weren't enough circus sessions to quench my thirst for juggling, so my parents would drop me off at Blossom's farmhouse and I would practice all day long. Admittedly, it might seem a little strange that a nine-year-old boy was allowed to go and hang out at a clown's house, when the clown didn't really know my parents that well and my parents didn't really know the clown; but hey, it was a different time. Besides, my parents had four kids so I guess they figured they could afford to lose one or two.

Years later, I asked Blossom (with whom I'm still in touch) and my parents about this and none of them were sure quite how this came about. Either my parents asked Blossom, "Hey can we leave our nine-year-old with you regularly for hours on end?", or Blossom asked my parents, "Hey, you should leave your nine-year-old with me regularly for hours on end?" I don't know. Either way, it was crazy and I loved it!

Blossom was always very supportive and encouraging towards me and my work. In true

34

Blossom style, she guffawed when I mentioned that I was writing this book. She is great and I wouldn't be where I am today without her, or my parents' liberal encouragement.

During a dusty day of practice down at the farm, I asked Blossom if she could teach me to juggle fire. She didn't say no. Instead, she responsibly said, "I'll need to call your parents". I imagine the conversation went a little like this:

Blossom:
Hi Denise! I'm here with your son and he's just asked me if I can teach him to juggle fire.

Denise (aka Mum):
Right...

Blossom:
Is that okay?

Denise (aka Mum):
Yeah, sure! I mean, he is almost ten...

Like I said, it was a different time.

For *F is for Forest*, my friend Anton was promoted from poster-boy to ABC Tour helper. When we arrived at the forest, the first hurdle was to get everything from the car to the forest.

Up to this point, show set-up hadn't been particularly difficult, but this time it was a complete nightmare.

We had two tables, a prop bag, a battery powered amplifier, a microphone and stand, and a light-box sign. Jennifer kindly lent us a small, all-terrain cart to lug the equipment over bumpy paths, tufts of grass and through murky puddles of thick mud.

As we headed from the open wet path into the forest, the atmosphere dramatically changed. A warm fire crackled in the distance and filled the air with smoke, candles in jars were delicately suspended from branches, the smell of stone soup (see endnote) wafted through the air, the frisson of excitable children and adults anticipating what was to come filled our ears, leaves crunched underfoot and the dregs of the day's sunlight peeped through the leaves. Ironically, the atmosphere was electric.

The show started with me appearing from backstage (behind a tree). The children from the forest school had gathered on logs, with their parents sitting behind them by the fire, all eagerly awaiting the show. They were such a generous and enthusiastic bunch that the show, despite its challenges, was actually a breeze.

At one point, I juggled the cups of water as I did at *E is for Eden Project*, the act where I drenched my nephew. I made a quick judgement call and assumed that the outdoorsy personalities of the forest school kids wouldn't mind a slight soaking either. Luckily, I was right, but that's probably a risk I shouldn't take too often.

For the finale, I juggled fire around the campfire. It was quite the novelty to be able to light my fire torches from the campfire itself.

Before the show, I had noticed that everybody was sitting around three quarters of the fire's circumference, so I went for the obvious choice and positioned myself in the remaining quarter so that the rest of the audience could see me. That kind of insight can only be learned from years of showbiz experience, I'll have you know.

Unfortunately, I soon realised that this quarter was unoccupied due to the direction of the wind, so I performed the entire set with smoke from the campfire billowing directly into my face. Damn you showbiz. If only I had gone to forest school. Despite this, and the challenge of getting to the campsite in the first place, the show went really well. The ABC Tour was finally starting to attract some real interest. At least, that's what I thought…

Stone Soup

Stone soup is a European folk story about some travellers who came to a village with no food, just a cooking pot. When they arrived, the villagers didn't want to share any of their food with the pesky travellers. The selfish gits. The clever travellers instead went to a river and filled their pot with water, plopped a large stone in it, then placed the pot on a fire. A passing villager became curious at their – quite frankly – insane behaviour and asked what they were doing.

The travellers told the villager that they were making stone soup, which is delicious, and that they'd be happy to share it, but that it needed a little bit of garnish, which they were missing, to improve the flavour.

The villager fell for the ruse and, eager to share some delightful soup, didn't mind parting with a couple of carrots, which were then bunged in. Another villager walked by, fell for the same nonsense as the first villager, and ended up parting with some seasoning. More villagers passed and fell for the con until the pot was filled with lots of food. The stone was then removed by the travellers and the soup was shared with everyone.

The moral is all about sharing – but I am sure that you got that.

G IS FOR GALLERY

Photos: Aaron Davies

Getting ideas from social media for 'F' was an accidental stroke of genius, so we continued with it for the rest of The ABC Tour. This benefitted the tour in a number of different ways:

1. It gave me a bunch of ideas for places that I could perform the show – these were usually a mixed bag but there were always a few gems in there.

2. It gave people the chance to feel part of the creative process of putting the tour together.

3. It kept people interested in the tour between shows, giving them a reason to interact and think creatively. With variable gaps between performances, this was ideal for keeping the overall momentum of the tour.

Honestly, I already knew that I wanted to perform in a gallery and had already looked into it, but I still put out the call for suggestions on social media.

Sometimes I really had no ideas for venues and was keen to get as many suggestions as possible. The majority of the time I already had a place in mind, and sometimes even a date and venue set in the diary. Very rarely, I would have an idea of somewhere I'd love to perform, then when I asked for suggestions, someone would come up with something far better than my original idea, in which case I would change my mind.

After an awkward phone call with the Tate Gallery (one of the most famous galleries in the world), I decided I needed to lower my expectations. The staff at the Tate didn't strictly

say no to me, but they did say that they only book events up to three and a half years in advance. It was time for me to go small and think local.

I ended up choosing a delightful little gallery located in the heart of Bristol called Hours Space. After *F is for Forest*, I had cranked up the online promotion for The ABC Tour by another couple of notches. I had even been interviewed by an online Bristol magazine called *Bristol 24/7* about the tour and the upcoming show.

As well as this, I had done interviews on *BBC Radio Bristol* and *Ujima Radio*, which were perfectly timed to promote *G is for Gallery*. The show would be free entry but attendees could pay what they wanted on the way out. All of the money raised would go towards a charity selected by Hours Space: they chose Borderlands, a fantastic organisation that helps refugees and asylum seekers.

Let's just quickly recap for emphasis.

- An article in Bristol 24/7.
- An interview on BBC Radio Bristol.
- An interview on Ujima Radio.
- Facebook advertising to promote the show.
- A venue in the centre of Bristol, one of the largest cities in the UK.
- Free entry.
- Charity event.

There were a lot of positives, and I had every reason to be optimistic that this show was going to be a groovy success.

On the day of the show, it was raining big buckets. Things got off to a rocky start pretty early on when I scratched my car on a wall trying to get into a tight space outside the venue. Annoying and frustrating, but I was adamant not to let it get to me.

Soaked through, I loaded the equipment into the gallery and began to transform it into a workable venue. Showtime soon came around and, despite the car scratch and the rain, my glass of cheer was still more than half full.

The audience trickled in slowly: when I say trickled, I mean eleven sodden people showed up. Two of them were from the charity, one was a friend that had agreed to take photos and six of them had seen the show before. Then there were two others, one of whom was an old

friend that I had bumped into earlier that day and invited to the show. She had brought her friend along.

This old friend was someone that I had a crush on in school. Even though I was in a relationship at the time of the show, I still really wanted her to walk away from the show thinking, *Wow, I hadn't seen Jon in a while. He's really doing great things with his life* [5].

---

[5] *A similar thing happened a few years earlier with another school crush, 'Beth' (I've used the name 'Beth' in order to keep Sarah's identity anonymous). 'Beth' was commonly known as one of the coolest and hottest girls in our school year, and I hadn't seen her since I was seventeen.*
I had a bizarre gig at a popular cosmetics shop in Oxford Street, London. It was the opening of the new store and a lot of acts – including myself – were booked to do shows inside the store throughout the day. We all had to arrive painstakingly early – before the store opened – so we could do a technical rehearsal on the stage.
The big boss of the event saw me practising inside and asked if I wouldn't mind doing that in front of the store to spike a bit of interest. I went out onto London's Oxford Street at the crack of dawn and started juggling. Unsurprisingly, there was nobody around: it was like a ghost town.
I followed my orders and stayed out there practising for a while and, to be honest, it was quite nice! While I was juggling I recognised a familiar face in the distance: school crush 'Beth' – 250 miles away from our Cornish school grounds – was walking down the street towards me.
Even though I was in my mid-twenties and my career was going swimmingly, all of those adolescent nerves suddenly came flooding back.
We both mustered out an awkward hello, but nothing more. As far as she was concerned, the guy that was obsessed with juggling in school hadn't grown up out of his childish hobby and was now clearly juggling on the street in the early hours begging for money. It didn't paint me in a good light.

After all that advertising, giving interviews for articles etc... hardly anyone came. It was heart wrenching. The show went okay, but definitely not great. There was nothing special about it. I'd personally give it two stars, but unfortunately, people don't like it when you write your own reviews.

After the show, I packed up, had a quick drink with the audience and then went to my car. I closed the door and had a little cry. This was a bad day. I was upset at a mixture of things. The main one was the small turnout for the show, especially after putting so much time and effort into promoting the damned thing. I had thought that, by this point in the tour, the concept might have gained a little more traction – but I was clearly wrong. I was also hit with the fact that I still had nineteen shows left and each one seemed to be getting progressively trickier.

Sitting alone in my scratched car, in the rain, was the first time where I wished I'd never started the tour and contemplated quitting. Yet as much as I wanted to, I couldn't just stop. I'd started it and managed to get this far, so I simply had to keep going. Quitting just wasn't an option.

Reflecting back on this gig, I wish I had done a better performance. It was just a gig in a gallery after all, and even though there were only eleven people in the audience, the show could have been so much better. I learned from later shows in the tour that small audiences (sometimes as small as two!), can be great.

I have some thoughts as to how I could improve the show if I had the chance to perform in a gallery again. One idea would be to have some ceramics specifically made, maybe a vase or a pot, and have it displayed on an open cabinet.

At the end of the show, one of my juggling props would "accidentally" knock it off of the cabinet so that it smashes on to the ground. I'd run out of the gallery, never to be seen again. The audience would look at what they think is a destroyed piece of artwork, on an empty stage. I'd love to have secretly filmed their reactions after I fled the scene.

Alternatively, I'd have a painting made. I'd then perform my water juggling routine close to it so that the water "accidentally" splashed onto the canvas, causing the paint to run. Then I'd scamper off like a devilish imp leaving the audience to squirm in the tension. Muahahah.

Mistakes are invaluable in life, as long as you don't make the same mistake twice. Luckily, I still had nineteen shows left, which gave me plenty of opportunities to apply what I'd learnt so far on the tour and make up for this show being below par. Onwards and upwards.

NOTE

'Beth', if you ever read this, I think you're cool, but not as cool as juggling. Just saying.

H IS FOR HAIRDRESSER'S

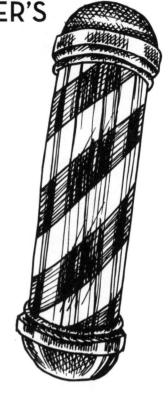

Having recovered from the grief of *G is for Gallery*, it was time for me to pull up my socks and crack on. For a long time I'd had my heart set on performing in a hairdresser's, but only for one, quite specific reason – I loved the idea of being sat with the hair protective cape on and having my hair cut and styled as the audience arrived. Then, with my do looking slick and stylish, I'd whip off the cape to reveal myself, suited and booted to the nines, ready for show time.

I pictured it a bit like a James Brown reveal with his cape, except with no backing dancers in hot-pants. This was essentially the only reason I wanted to perform in a hairdresser's and, if I'm honest, I didn't plan beyond the funky introduction. There were other possibilities for 'H', but my stubborn mind was already set. Possibly because my feelings were still damaged from the *G is for Gallery* experience, and I didn't want to make things too difficult for myself. Deep down, I knew that performing in a hairdresser's would be easy, and there would certainly be one in Bristol that would be up for it.

Despite hankering for *H is for Hairdresser's*, I still received several good ideas on social media that could have made the cut:

HANGAR

A nice idea but I didn't know of one nearby

HOSPITAL

When I was in the hospital for my appendectomy, I wouldn't have wanted someone trying to entertain me, let alone film me!

HELIPAD

Could be a bit draughty

HOTEL

I spend a lot of my life in hotels – and not by choice. I didn't want to spend more time in one.

HOME

I didn't want the audience knowing where I live.

HIPPO ENCLOSURE

Hippos are the most dangerous animal in Africa. It would also be 'E for Enclosure'

My mind was set. It was time to book a hair appointment.

I heard about a fancy, hipster hairdresser's in town called Shotgun Barbers. I had learnt from earlier gigs, that it was better to approach people face to face rather than engage in an awkward phone conversation along the following lines:

Venue:
We don't really do shows here.

Me:
I know. That's why I want to do a show there.

Venue:
I don't get it.

For some reason, this conversation always went a lot better face to face. With that in mind, I nipped down to the hairdresser's. As I walked inside, I noticed the record player spinning, the barbers cutting fashionably asymmetrical cuts, the funky décor, and the flat white coffees on the table. I had entered hipster heaven and had a hunch that whoever ran this joint would be game.

I was introduced to the manager – a tall, pale guy with bleach blond, cool-dude hair called Sam Young – who listened intently to what I had to say. Before I had even reached the end of my (by now) well-practiced ABC Tour spiel, he was asking me when I'd like to perform and how he could help. This was music to my ears.

When Anton and I turned up on the day of the show, Sam was in the salon and eager to help. We immediately noticed the *H is for Hairdresser's* poster in the window. His support was very welcome after the catastrophe of *G is for Gallery*. Sam was there, holding The ABC Tour up on much appreciated scaffolding poles.

Together, we arranged the old school swivel barber chairs for the audience to sit on, and then faced them towards the back of the room where a perforated metal sign with a flying duck on it acted as the backdrop for the stage. Combining our lights and the lights around the mirrors, we illuminated the space and created a rather marvellous looking venue.

As predicted, other than getting my hair cut as the audience arrived[6] and then being revealed like the Juggling Godfather of Soul himself, the show wasn't particularly adventurous. The audience laughed and cheered at all of the

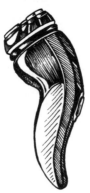

appropriate times and the performance went down a treat, but I couldn't help but feel that I'd slightly cheated again.

I'd taken the path of least resistance by choosing an easy venue to perform in. Worse still, I hadn't even challenged myself to create any new material for it.

Apart from the free haircut at the top of the show, there was nothing particularly unusual about the performance. It just felt like a regular gig that I could have done anywhere. That would have been fine for any other tour, but for this one, it kind of defeated the point.

I definitely learned that, from this show onwards, I would have to make the shows more challenging for myself and make sure that the performances going forwards were specifically designed to reflect the venue.

The good thing about picking an easy option for 'H', was that it gave me the massive confidence boost that I'd needed to mend my relationship with The ABC Tour, after the beast of *G is*

---

[6] *I was delighted to unexpectedly spot a familiar face in the crowd that I hadn't seen for almost fifteen years: Agi Macleay. At ten years old, I started working for Agi in a company called Jungle Bungle Jugglers. During weekends and school holidays we would perform in holiday parks all over Cornwall. I worked with them on and off for almost six years. Despite not seeing Agi for many years, it was like we had never parted. If it wasn't for Agi and her support in the early days, I am not sure I would have ever reached where I am today. I owe massive thanks to Agi. She truly is an exceptional egg.*

Photo: Anton Mackman

Photo: Anton Mackman

for Gallery thumped me right in the guts. *H is for Hairdresser's* invigorated me once more and gave me the drive to keep going.

During the show I performed my helium balloon juggling routine, which finishes with the release of some of the balloons up towards the ceiling. After the gig, as we packed up, we tried to work out how to get the helium balloons back down.

Over the years I've learnt that they must come down before I leave, otherwise they tend to descend during the night and set off security alarms. I didn't want that to happen,

especially as Shotgun Barbers had been so accommodating. After a lot of trial and error I have developed a foolproof way to safely retrieve helium balloons from the ceiling. Firstly, fill another balloon to the maximum with helium and then attach it to a roll of ribbon. Secondly, stick double-sided tape (or just regular tape folded over) all around the circumference of the balloon.

Thirdly, release it up to the ceiling, towards the other balloons, so that they stick to the tape on the balloon on the end of your ribbon. Finally, gently pull the balloons down together in a clump. You may have to do this a few times but it hasn't failed me yet. It is also incredibly fun because it is like fishing from the sky! A top tip there for whenever you are next in that particular situation. You're very welcome.

As I was attaching the tape to the balloon for my foolproof, tried-and-tested technique, I heard Sam say that he had a better method. He promptly went downstairs to get something. Better? I thought. Better than my technique that I had spent a lot of time and effort developing? But hey, I thought, I'd give him the benefit of the doubt.

Sam returned holding an air-powered BB shotgun[7] and aimed it towards the ceiling; before we had time to get to safety, he started firing. The pellets ricocheted around the room a gazillion times – off the ceiling, floor, walls, mirrors – occasionally being intercepted by an innocent helium balloon who never stood a chance. It was quite a terrifying, but rather amusing, end to a delightful evening. Sadly, none of the balloons lived to tell the tale.

---

[7] *I guess that's why it's called Shotgun Barbers*

I IS FOR INTERNET

L–R: Bobby May, Albert Lucas, Trixie

Illustration: Darryl J Carrington

I knew that, having gotten The ABC Tour back on track with *H is for Hairdresser's*, I needed to up the ante and start challenging myself more. My first thought was to perform somewhere with ice so I'd have the challenge of facing the cold, armed with nothing but my usual arsenal of juggling props.

I looked online and found a fantastic bar in London called the Ice Bar[8] where all of the décor – including the seats and even the glasses for the drinks – were made out of ice.

The venue looked beautiful so I gave them a call. I received a flat-out refusal, and they added that they would never have anything like that in their "prestigious" venue. I understood that they weren't interested, but I felt that their response was a bit cold[9].

With The ABC Tour being too hot for the Ice Bar to handle, I had to hit my Plan B: Ice rink. I have always been interested in performing on ice skates, as there has been a long line of professional jugglers that have done just this.

---

[8] *I know, I know. If I follow my own stupid rules, Ice Bar is technically B is for Bar. But whatever.*

[9] *Because it's an Ice Bar. HAHAHAHAHAHAHAHAHAHAHAHAHAHAHAHAHAHAHAHAHAHA!*

On ice skates, Trixie Larue would juggle six plates whilst bouncing a ball on her head, Bobby May would perform technical three club routines, and Albert Lucas performed a combination trick consisting of spinning a ring on his leg, balancing a ball on a stick in his mouth, and juggling nine rings while standing on one skate!

The difference between these legends and me is that, firstly, they were better jugglers, and secondly, they could ice skate. But maybe, just maybe, I could learn to perform my show – or at least a version of my show – on ice, once I had some basic training. My naiveté was pretty clear in hindsight, but I fell victim to the optimism that tends to define me and thought: How hard could it be?

The truth is, it was pretty bloody hard. Learning to ice skate, and then learning to do a show on ice skates, was just the first issue I faced. The next part of the challenge would be to convince an ice rink to let me do a show. Here are a few hurdles that came up:

1. Health and Safety
Health and safety. They would ask if I'd done this before. I would say no. Then they would get concerned, thinking that I might seriously injure myself. They had a fair point.

2. When I Could Perform
I'd have to perform on the ice when there was no one else skating because if I dropped anything, then people might trip over it. Therefore I'd need an empty ice rink with people watching from the sides.

3. Audience Considerations
An empty ice rink when people are around usually means that people want to skate, and then my show would be eating into their skating time. Not cool.

I started contacting ice rinks to see if I could persuade them to let me do a show. None of them went for it, so I decided that I'd try and sell the same thing but from a different angle. A friend told me that his local ice rink hosted ice hockey events. I contacted the next ice rink on my ever-shortening list and asked them about any future ice hockey games. They said there was one in a couple of months, so then I offered to do the halftime entertainment for free.

An offer they couldn't refuse, right? Wrong. They could, and they did. However, they did offer a spot on the rink to do my show, between the fun skating session for the public and the ice hockey game in the evening. I would perform for the general public who had just finished their skating session. *I is for Ice Rink* was officially booked.

At this point, you may be thinking that I have incorrectly titled this chapter. I haven't. Be patient.

After confirming *I is for Ice Rink*, Anton designed the poster and we started promoting the show. I also sent the poster to the Ice Rink so that they could start promoting it on their end. The next challenge was to learn to ice skate – and I had just under two months.

I called on my Swedish/Finnish friend, Lynda Musgrove, who worked at a local rink, to teach me. After a couple of sessions, I began to grasp the magnitude of the challenge. Lynda was a great teacher, but I was not a natural skater. I could just about force out a shaky three club juggle, but I was no Trixie.

The more I skated, the more I doubted that I could learn enough in time to not make a complete klutz of myself. Luckily, the closer I got to the ice skating gig, the less they replied to my emails about logistics and promotion. It was a week before the event, and I hadn't heard anything from them for a month. I had called, left voice messages, tried contacting them on social media, and still no reply. I checked the website to see if *I is for Ice Rink* was advertised as one of their events and it was not.

The night before the show, I left them a stern voice message, saying that I wouldn't be turning up to do the show and that their lack of response had forced me to cancel. I had confirmed a date with them and they reconfirmed the date in an email, but then they seemed to vanish into thin air! It was almost as if the person I had spoken to at the venue didn't even work there and had just popped in for the day to answer a few calls and cause merry havoc.

This was particularly gutting as I'd put a lot of time into promotion, as well as learning to ice skate. Not only does a cancellation on a tour like this cause an inconvenience in the sense of having to book another venue, it also significantly delays the whole tour. It was mishaps like this that meant that The ABC Tour took two years to complete.

Ironically, with *I is for Ice Rink* having been cancelled, I found myself standing on thin ice. I already had 'J' booked in the diary, which was meant to be happening a week after *I is for Ice Rink*, and now I needed to find an alternative for 'I', and do so quickly in order to keep the shows in alphabetical order. I don't know why I felt the pressing need for the shows to be in order but, for some reason, this was very important to me.

Regretfully the time passed quickly as I was preparing for 'J'; this meant that 'I' ended up a few weeks after 'J' and was the first show performed out of sequence.

I needed to sort a last-minute venue for 'I'. My first thought – which I can imagine would be everybody's first thought in a situation like this – was to try and build an igloo. It was January, so it was quite cold, but there was no snow.

In my head, I would be able to build an igloo out of crushed ice from various peoples freezers etc. It's clear now that I was definitely going a bit insane and you'll be disappointed to hear that I didn't even attempt this genius igloo idea.

Luckily, at this point, my friend Courtney Prokopas entered into The ABC Tour's peripheral vision, wanting to get involved and offering her services by trying to make bookings, brainstorming ideas and generally assisting with whatever needed doing. At the time, she was over from America doing an MA for Directing Circus at Circomedia in Bristol.

She thought that maybe The ABC Tour could help towards her course, as she was researching performance for camera, and the uniqueness of person vs persona for circus performers.

We were chatting over coffee one day when she came up with the idea of me doing *I is for Internet*: a show online in the style of an interactive game-show. Honestly, I wasn't initially sold on the idea but she did a great job of cajoling me into it. I called up Anton and set a date that I could do it at his house, as he has the nicest house out of the people I know living nearby.

The poster was made, I published it online and then I was set. The only problem I had now was: how the hell do I do a show on the internet? I had about three days to figure it out.

It's worth saying that this show was a few years before Covid-19. During the many lockdowns of the pandemic, performers were forced to use their initiative to find ways to replicate a live performance online. At the time of *I is for Internet*, there were no online shows that I knew of, so I really had no idea how to do it at all. Nowadays, the concept of an online show feels like part of the repertoire for a lot of performers but, back then, we were stepping into unknown territory. In retrospect, The ABC Tour was clearly ahead of the curve by about 22 months.

I was lucky enough to be surrounded by people that could help me figure out this online show conundrum. New to the team was Dan Edwards, who is an exceptionally talented videographer. From this show onwards, Dan was the go-to guy for all of The ABC Tour shows. He has the ability to not only film fantastic footage but, with his special superpower of seeming to blend into the background like a camera-chameleon, one can often forget that Dan is even

there. This meant that he could film without any of us being aware, which made the footage all the more interesting and authentic.

After some brainstorming between Courtney, Anton and me, we decided that we'd do the show on Facebook through its Facebook Live function and that, as there would be no physical audience present, we needed to find creative ways to interact with viewers. With this loose plan in place, we each had our assigned jobs: Courtney would help with the set up and manage the show from the other side of the screen, Anton would read the chat comments during the show and relay any information to me that he thought was important or funny, Dan would sneakily film from the shadows, and I would perform.

Three days later, we were set up and ready to go at Anton's house but there was an unusual atmosphere in the air. I was about to do a show. Lights! Costume! Everything in place, apart from the audience. Normally, when I'm about to do a show I can hear the audience on the other side of the curtain, or even surreptitiously watch them come in. Their cacophony of chatter and excitement helps me get in the right mindset for the show: I thrive on it. But here, there was no noise. Just me and a couple of mates in Anton's house, about to do a show on the internet to – quite possibly – nobody at all.

To give people a chance to log on, we went live on Facebook and set a ten-minute timer on the screen as a countdown to the show. It was quite exciting to see the number of people watching gradually increase. I began by asking the viewers to share the link to the stream on their social media platforms. I repeated this several times throughout the show until, eventually, there were thousands following the live stream.

With no physical audience in the room, we decided that we needed to make it as interactive as possible, so that people would remain engaged. For example, I juggled three different coloured balloons and got the cyber audience to vote for which one they'd like me to pop. After the votes were counted up, I popped the balloon; inside was a piece of paper that had written on it the next section of the show that I had to perform.

One of my favourite ideas for this show came from Anton. There was a public telephone box outside of Anton's house. We gave the online audience the phone number and whoever called first could request a trick. I loved this part because it meant we had to take the laptop and cameras onto the street, which felt extra exciting. I really loved the surprise element of this show as it forced me to keep thinking on my feet.

During the show, Courtney had the idea of having another computer running a webcam website called Chat Roulette. For those of you more pure of heart and mind, Chat Roulette is a website where you can log on and turn on your webcam to somebody else in the world that is also on the platform at the same time. Once you are bored of that particular person, or they are bored of you, you simply click 'next' and you get through to another random person in the world. It's a fun idea. During the show, we had people from all over – Germany, Iraq, Italy – watching the show through Chat Roulette. Unfortunately, as there are a lot of filthy dirty monkey men in the world, most people that connected really felt the need to show us their penises.

As I was performing, I couldn't tell them what I really thought of them, so Courtney was on "wang watch" and had to keep clicking 'next' every time someone popped out their little fella. It is very off-putting to do a show whilst there is a computer in front of you showing a near-constant stream of sausage. Disturbingly, this wasn't the last bunch of willies that were on display during The ABC Tour.

Despite the sluice of schlongs, it was thrilling to perform to people from all over the world, each one watching from the comfort of their own homes. Never before have I done a show for as many people in different places at the same time.

What I really loved about this show was that it felt like a true collaboration compared to other stops along the tour. This definitely wouldn't have been possible to run with any fewer than four people. A true team effort.

J IS FOR JAIL

Johnny Cash was known for doing a lot of outlandish things, but one that always stuck in my mind was his tour of US prisons. There's a particular video of him performing "A Boy Named Sue" in Saint Quentin State Prison. The roars of appreciation, the rapport Cash had with the audience, and just how the song lyrics resonated with the raucous inmates watching: all of this combined to create a joyous yet slightly menacing atmosphere.

I knew that it would be a major inconvenience to film a show in a real jail, due to the bureaucracy and red tape involved, but as luck would have it, there is an old jail in the centre of Bristol called The Island, which can be hired for events.

Before confirming the booking, I was offered a site visit so I could suss out the venue. Tina Backhouse (my contact on the inside) guided me through the creepy corridors and cells that make up the jail. The conversation echoed off the cold walls as we walked.

At one point, I asked Tina if she could lock me in a particularly ominous looking cell so I could experience what it would be like to do time. I sat on the cold, uncomfortable bed as the door slammed shut and the key turned in the lock to seal me in. Gradually the bouncing echo faded out and I could hear Tina's footsteps getting quieter

as

      she

             wandered

                        off

down

      the   *corridor.*

All I could hear was stone cold, eerie silence.

After some time, my ears adjusted to hear nothing but the inner workings of my own body. My heart pumping blood around my various flumes. My body digesting the sandwich I'd eaten just before arriving.

I couldn't help but imagine the types of people that had, at one time, sat exactly where I was sitting. What had they done? What had they felt? Had they murdered? Maybe just

unpaid parking tickets? Or perhaps they were also just doing a site visit for their own juggling shows? The latter, I supposed, was unlikely. This quiet, cold, creepy, claustrophobic, clammy and – in all seriousness – anxiety-inducing space, was the perfect place for a challenging ABC Tour show.

After what felt like six years, I screamed for Tina to release me and she unlocked the doors, giggling, telling me I had only been in there for a couple of minutes. In all honesty, I don't think I am built for the clink.

J is for Jail was the first show that I had to fork out money to hire the venue. This meant that I had to sell tickets in order to cover my costs and, hopefully, make a small profit. I felt extra pressure, not only to ensure that the show was worth the money but also to put the word out to make sure a decent crowd attended.

In keeping with other shows on the tour, I went with the tried-and-tested-and-failed method of combining Facebook ads with some radio interviews to help get the word out. I wanted to offer a more immersive experience than in previous shows so I bought myself a bright orange prisoner's jumpsuit,

which I have to say, I felt particularly cool in.

In the lead-up to *J is for Jail*, I also spent a couple of days working out a routine specifically for this show. I dug out a pair of my old handcuffs and started putting together a juggling routine that I could perform while wearing them. I was delighted with how this turned out, so much so that handcuffed juggling might be something I revisit again in the future as part of my regular act.

I woke up on the day of the performance with a nose tightly packed with snot and the gravelly timbre of a long-time smoker (for the record, Mum, I have never smoked). Nonetheless, I was oozing with *joie de vivre* for the show.

Helping out once again was the multi-talented Anton, who was dressed up as the Jail Warden. As well as being a good friend, the designer of all but two of The ABC Tour posters, a videographer of many of the shows and a good juggler, he is also one half of a fantastic double act called "The 2 Men". "The 2 Men" – in their various guises – entertain crowds and cause havoc, most frequently while dressed as traffic wardens.

Photos: Anton Mackman

As Anton already had a traffic warden's outfit and some "Billy Bob Teeth", I thought it would be a great idea to use him as the Jail Warden, guiding people in and telling them where to sit.

The layout of the jail was quite unusual compared to other venues I'd performed in. There was a long, cold dead end of a corridor, with doors to three jail cells coming off it. Before you reached the corridor there was a large open space, somewhat like a foyer (I can't imagine that they'd call it that). Connecting the jail's "lobby" to the corridor beyond was a classic wall-to-ceiling barred gate. This meant we'd have to be inventive if we wanted to make the most out of the space's potential.

The original plan was to set out some chairs and lights in the Jail's reception (Lounge? Atrium?) and, as the music started, I would emerge from the depths of the darkened corridor, burst through the gate wearing my orange jumpsuit and handcuffs, and start the show.

Anton had an even better idea: instead of doing that introduction and then keeping the entire show in the ballroom of the jail, we could move the audience into the various cells for different parts of the show.

While I was enthused by this, with less than an hour until showtime I was struggling to get my snot-filled head around the logistics.

Ushering the audience throughout the show posed more than a few difficulties. First off, we'd have to move the sound equipment between rooms as we went, which would be a bit of a hassle. Secondly, the cells themselves were pretty small. If the audience was inside, I'd have less than half a metre of performance space to work with. This meant that the chance of someone being hit by a stray juggling prop was exceptionally high.

Luckily for me, among his myriad of talents, Anton is also a top class problem solver. As the warden, he figured he'd be able to move the sound equipment while ushering people between the cells, which would make the transitions a lot smoother.

His solution to the other problem was less reassuring. As I recall, his words were something like, "Don't worry, there'll be loads of room. You could fit a bus in there! Just... do your best not to hit anyone, okay?"

With our new solutions at the ready, the audience soon arriving and my anxiety levels shooting through the

roof, I hid out of sight down the end of the corridor. It was a cold January evening, in the UK, in a jail cell. To stay warm, I was doing my pre-show jumping jacks and I could see my own breath.

One last gulp of my honey-and-lemon-based flu relief drink, and it was time to start. Deep breath in, and exhale like a vapist. Adjusting my orange jumpsuit, I started the music, slapped the handcuffs on and kicked open the gate. It made a much louder noise than I had anticipated and caused the audience to jump. Perhaps I took the old showbiz advice of "start the show with a BANG!" a bit too literally.

It was surprising to see that a decent crowd had actually come to the gig. It was freezing cold and they were all wrapped up like a family of Inuit. They had no idea what to expect and had paid good money to come and spend their evening with a juggler in a jail. I just hoped that none of them were claustrophobic.

I threw myself into the opening handcuff routine with all the enthusiasm I could muster. Perhaps with a little too much gusto. As I threw the first ball, the handcuffs constricted to their tightest setting and dug in hard against my wrist.

This was not the plan. As the crooked and kinky would know, once you tighten handcuffs they do not loosen. I had three minutes left of juggling to do, and the handcuffs had already dug into my flesh enough to leave marks that I'd later have to explain. I struggled through this routine and released myself from the cuffs as soon as I could.

With the first quarter of the show complete, the audience was herded into the first cell by Anton the Jail Warden and I performed the easiest of my three jail cell sets. From this point onwards, the risk level went up from cell to cell, as each room decreased in size and the space needed for the material I was performing grew larger. A monumental planning error.

After Anton ushered the crowd into the cells, he slammed the door closed to leave us trapped in together for each mini performance. I waited, letting the sound of the slam reverberate around the room until it was deathly silent.

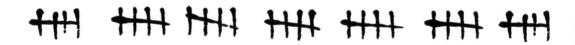

60

This was a different kind of uncomfortable than when I was locked in the cell by myself. Having a group of people with me made it drastically more claustrophobic and, in turn, this ramped up the excitement. The air felt thicker. The audience was crammed into a cell with people they didn't know, and was clearly unsure about what was going to happen. It was like we were on a set of a B-list horror-movie but with the mood undercut by the frivolity of juggling and jokes.

In Cell Two I performed a bounce juggling routine inspired by my favourite juggling company, Gandini Juggling. Gandini Juggling plays a monumental part in my career. I would not be a professional juggler if not for them. In fact, when I was eighteen, I was training to be an electrician! Even then, I juggled a lot and I had no passion for electronics at all. My plan was to spend three years becoming an electrician and then I'd have that as a back up whilst I tried to make a career in juggling.

Six months into my electrical apprenticeship (where I was earning £80 a week), I got a phone call from Sean Gandini (co-founder of Gandini Juggling with Kati Ylä-Hokkala) asking if I'd like to do a show with them for one week in London. I lost my mind. This was a dream come true. I asked my boss for permission to take the time off of work, and he said no. I asked, "What would you do if I went anyway?". He replied, "I'd fire you!". I went home that day frustrated. After speaking to my parents about it, I asked them what I should do, and they said, "Call his bluff! Go to London and do the gig. Come back and just go into work as if nothing happened". My parents are amazing.

I had an extraordinary time working with Gandini Juggling that week performing a show called The Big Water Juggle, that took place in the

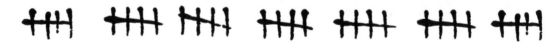

fountains of Somerset House, in London. At the end of it, I had a chat with Sean and he said that, if I wanted to, I could make a career as a juggler in London and he would chuck some gigs my way. He doesn't know this, but that was a life-changing conversation for me.

I returned to Cornwall, went into work, and was promptly fired. It was the best – and only – firing that I've ever received. I then started saving money to go to London six months later with my parents' blessing, under the condition that I would try and be a juggler for a year and, if it didn't work out, I would come back and finish the electrical apprenticeship.

I did everything I could to prevent this fate, including kids' parties, stilt walking, fire juggling, and all of the other things I hate doing. Despite my distaste of them, they are still a million times better than crawling through rat poop and itchy insulation in the small roof cavities of old houses for a measly £80 a week.

Spoiler alert: the juggling thing worked out in the end.

I have worked on various shows with Gandini Juggling over the past twelve years and one show of theirs that I have always loved is The Cube.

The Cube was performed in a see-through, tempered glass cube approximately the size of a prison cell, so it could be viewed from every angle. The juggler would climb inside through a trapdoor in the ceiling, and perform a routine with bouncing balls, rebounding them off the floor and perpendicular walls. It created a fantastic effect as the balls zoomed around the juggler like speeding planets orbiting the sun. I wanted to create this effect in Cell Two, except the audience would be watching the show from inside the cube/cell with me, as opposed to outside the cube/cell where it is nice and safe and no one can be struck by a wayward juggling ball.

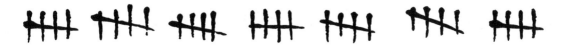

Before I started the routine, I got the audience to verbally agree that they wouldn't mind (or sue me!) if they got hit with a prop. I think this is about as good as a legally binding contract, right? With the audience sitting either side of me on raised seating, and a "stage" running the length of a cell approximately half a metre wide, I then proceeded to throw balls against the walls, both in front of and behind the assembled crowd. Balls ricocheted off the clammy walls that the back row was leaning against, sometimes irresponsibly striking the wall only a few inches above their heads. Reckless, unprofessional, dangerous, intimidating, and scary – but what a buzz! I can confirm that no audience members were hurt during the performance of this show. At least none that are allowed to talk about it. Legally binding![10]

By the time we got to the final mini performance in Cell Three, the audience was a lot more relaxed.

Instead of deathly silence after the metal door slammed, there was a murmur of giggles. As I mentioned, each cell was smaller than the last, and Cell Three gave me very little room to work in.

On one side of the cell was a hard wooden bed with no mattress, and on the other was a disconnected toilet. I performed up on the bed, with most of the audience sitting on benches – and one lucky person having the privilege of sitting on the throne. This was a particularly sketchy section to perform, as I was juggling clubs and the audience were so close that some of the action was happening inches above their heads. Fear not; I legally had my back covered. Who knew that legal issues could be solved so easily?

On the wall of the cell a tally had been kept, presumably where someone had been counting down the days, weeks, months or years until their release back into the wider world. I had planned ahead and had

---

[10] *Once I was performing a Gandini Juggling gig in Dubai. We were there for two weeks, and they wanted me and another juggler, John Blanchard, to perform in The Cube. As it was too inconvenient to get The Cube over to Dubai, they built a custom-made replica, which was exactly the same as the original Cube, except that it was completely different and not very good. Soon I was performing The Cube daily with Blanchard, throwing balls around each other. However, it was left outside all day in the relentless Dubai sun (around 40°C), drawing in heat like a greenhouse. Opening the door was like opening an oven. After five minutes in The Cube, we would come out drenched from head to toe in sweat. It was bad. But that was still not as bad as being an electrical apprentice.*

a pen in my pocket, and scheduled a deliberate drop into the club juggling section. When the club hit the ground, I would take the pen out and add another dash to the tally. It's a shame that this is a joke that I can't replicate anywhere else.

The show finished with some really great feedback from the audience. Despite the cold and the constant danger of death, maiming or decapitation, they had clearly considered it money well spent[11].

I particularly enjoyed doing this show because it was tough to put together and we had to come up with some interesting concepts to make the most out of the situation. Even better, I was able to perform material in the jail that I wouldn't have been able to perform anywhere else.

This was the eye-opening moment when I realised what I really wanted The ABC Tour to be about. It was an opportunity for me to try out new, location-specific material in very unusual and challenging places.

No longer was I going to look for the easy cop-out options that had marked the first run of shows on the tour. *T is for Theatre*? No way. *S is for Stage*? I don't think so. I had a feeling that, from this moment on, things were going to be trickier and more stressful, and it would be nobody's fault but my own.

---

[11] *I later found out that J is for Jail was a first date for a couple called Emma and Finn. At the time of writing, they are still happily together. I love the fact that The ABC Tour has resulted in at least one happy relationship. Unlike a lot of relationships, books last forever. So no pressure on Emma and Finn, but I've written this now and printed it. So, if you could be nice to each other and stay together – not for me, not for each other, but for the sake of the consistency of the book's narrative – then that would be just great. I'll reward you with a 10% discount on this book as an incentive. Cheers in advance.*

K IS FOR KNITTING CLUB

Knowing that 'K' would be an issue, I started thinking about this one early on. It's tough to think of any venue for 'K' that fits the rules. Try it. Go on. Try it now. I'll wait. Did you do it? No? I knew it! Go on, off you pop. Stop reading and focus on thinking of a venue for 'K'. It's tough, isn't it? Here are some suggestions that the delightful social media elves came up with:

KENNELS

I'm not 100% sure but I think a kennel is a bit like a dog shelter. I'd already barked up that tree to no avail.

KERNOW

Kernow means 'Cornwall' in Cornish, for those not fluent in a dead language. While it's a marvellous place, it's still a place name.

KIDS' PARTY

I respect anyone that can perform for kids but I am personally just not very good at it. This is also technically P is for Party.

KEBAB SHOP

This is S is for Shop, unless I performed in a massive kebab. I wasn't against that option!

KITCHEN

A strong contender – but it's definitely been done before by circus artists dressed as chefs, juggling food and kitchen utensils.

KINDERGARTEN

Like Kids' Party, it would've been a great idea for this tour to see me go through the struggle of trying to control an audience of toddlers.

A few years ago, I performed at the Thursford Christmas Spectacular in Norfolk. This was an eight-week contract with a huge cast of dancers, singers, musicians and I was the speciality act. It is quite possibly the most Christmassy place one can imagine – even more so than taking The Polar Express to the set of A Muppets' Christmas Carol. Thursford is all of this on steroids, with the festive dial cranked up to eleven.

During the contract, I noticed that a lot of the cast were knitting in between shows and rehearsals to pass the time. One of the singers asked me if I'd like to try and knit a square, which would then be added to a blanket to be auctioned off for charity at the end of the contract. I agreed. Here is the said blanket. Can you guess which square is mine?

I also gave myself the challenge of knitting a scarf during my time at Thursford and found the whole process rather enjoyable. Before rehearsals or shows, the green room backstage would be filled with people knitting a variety of items, whilst socialising and drinking endless cups of tea. This scene always filled me with warmth, and gave me the idea for *K is for Knitting Club*. I loved the thought of performing to an audience of people that were knitting. It just seemed really lovely to me.

Now before we go any further, I am aware that I have broken another rule. *K is for Knitting Club*, really should be *C is for Club*, right? Yes, you are right. But at least it is phonetically correct. Also, I liked the idea too much to worry about continuity. I would say it is less of a rule broken, and more of a rule bruised or slightly grazed.

Before I could start my search for a knitting club, I needed to define what one was. Is it just a group of people knitting? Does this mean the location doesn't matter? If people are knitting in a church, is that a knitting club? I think yes. If they are knitting outside in a field, is that a knitting club? This feels like a no. If they are knitting in an office, is this a knitting club? I think yes. If they are knitting at a bus shelter, is this a knitting club? I think not.

Does this mean that it only qualifies as a knitting club if it is fully enclosed within four walls? This must be the case. If ten people are knitting in a room, is this a club? I think so. If two people are knitting in a room, is this a club? I'm not sure. I think not, unless it is a club with poor attendance that particular week.

So, to find my venue for *K is for Knitting Club*, I was on the lookout for at least three people knitting in a room that is enclosed on all sides.

With my keyboard waxed, I surfed the web for knitting clubs in my local area. My process was to email ten knitting clubs about the tour and inform them that I'd love to do a show at their club for free. If they liked, they could sell tickets and raise money for a charity of their choice, or for their club. Surely, this would work. They'd all reply saying, "Yes please! Pick us! Pick us!!! Let's set a date right now!". Then I would choose the closest one to my house, set a date and move on. Easy peasy lemon squeezy.

Dear reader, let me tell you something that I am sure you already know. It was far from easy. It wasn't lemon squeezy. I had the same issues that I'd experienced with 'D' – when I thought that I could easily squeezily book a dog shelter to perform at. That wound was open, and the lemon was being squeezilied inside. The majority of knitting clubs didn't reply, and the rest plainly said that they weren't interested.

Now, I know that I am biased towards juggling: personally I love it, and always have. I am aware that it isn't for everyone. I know there will be people reading this book that love juggling. Then there will be the rest of you who are probably reading this book because it was a gift from someone that loves juggling or thinks that you love juggling. Perhaps you are reading this because you love alphabets and feel ambivalent towards juggling at best. If so, I apologise for the lack of alphabet-related content. That being said, if I am running a club of any type, and a stranger contacts me to offer a free show involving something I have no interest in – but could help raise money for my club or my chosen charity – then I would absolutely say yes. But I am also the type of person that would willingly choose to do twenty-six awkward shows in difficult venues for free.

Through a suggestion from a friend, I managed to get in touch with Kate Evans, who works at a company called Immediate Media that publishes knitting magazines such as *Simply Knitting*, *The Knitter*

and *You've Got Knits* (I may have made one of those up). After pitching the idea to her, she was immediately on board. Immediate Media have their own knitting club where employees will regularly meet up for a little knittle. There was the added bonus of Kate being able to advertise the show in advance through the company's knitting magazines. It smelt like a delicious recipe for success, so the date was stitched into the diary, a poster was crocheted and the advertising campaign was sewn up.

The show was booked to take place in the Immediate Media canteen, which is located in a tower block in the centre of Bristol. This meant that when the audience would arrive for the show, they would have to give their names to the security guard in the reception, who would check them off the list and give them directions to the venue. The image of random members of the public getting directions and security clearance to the juggling show taking place in a knitting club really tickled me. A classic ABC Tour moment.

On the day of the show, Anton and I had one hour to transform the canteen into a venue fit for a juggling and comedy show at a knitting club. I was adamant that it needed to look like a knitting club, even though I didn't know what that meant (other than having four walls and three knitters). It is amazing how something as simple as setting out some chairs, turning on a couple of industrial lights and scattering balls of wool around the place transformed the room from a canteen to a bone fide venue. A week prior to the show, my talented friend, Laura Curry, had even knitted a woolly cover for my mic stand which really helped tie it all together.

The audience arrived and soon there were more needles being prepared than a coronavirus vaccination clinic. It was great to look into the audience and see so many occupied hands being taken up with needlework. What I didn't anticipate was the issue that arose from encouraging the audience to knit throughout the show, whilst also asking them to clap if they saw something worth applauding. I was giving two opposing commands which must have been very confusing for them. *Knit, Clap, Knit, Clap, Knit, Clap.* Try saying this really fast. It's the first – and probably last – tongue twister of the book. I only realised I'd done this about two hours after the show had finished. What a knit wit.

Despite the woolly and muffled applause, the show went tremendously well. There were two parts that I was particularly pleased with. The first was a trick that I had always wanted to perform but had never found the right context for it. It is a trick with the diabolo, which is like a large yoyo, but it is controlled with two sticks connected with a piece of string. Firstly, you get the diabolo spinning really fast, and then you place it on a different long piece of string and let it spin along the entire length before catching it off of the other end.

To do this, we obviously used wool. Halfway through my diabolo routine, I ran through the audience to the back of the room where Anton held the preset wool up high and ready to go. As planned, I spun the living heckers out of the diabolo and placed it on the string. The diabolo then zoomed at the rate of an arthritic tortoise back towards the stage, and over the audiences' heads, where I was there to retrieve it off of the wool and back into the diabolo routine without a stitch[12].

---

[12] *This moment was reminiscent of when my brother Steve, my next-door neighbours Matt and Chris, and I would play with diabolos out on the street as kids. We would aim to toss the diabolos high into the air so that they'd land on the telephone wire where they would spin and slide all the way down into an old man's garden. He'd begrudgingly return them. Then we'd do it again. A good time was had by all.*

Photos: Dan Edwards

The other segment I was thrilled to perform wasn't a trick of my own but was instead created by Jay Gilligan, who, as I've mentioned before, is one of my all-time favourite jugglers. Jay first inspired me with juggling when I was fifteen years old at Glastonbury Festival. He came out on stage in the circus big top to rock music, and performed some of the most punk-rock, avant-garde juggling that I had ever seen, while wearing just jeans and a t-shirt. All the juggling I had ever seen up until that point was performed by people wearing bow ties, with their hair combed, shirts tucked in, polished shoes, usually performing along to swing music. Jay broke the rules and at this time of my life, it was exactly what I needed to see. Jay is still creating prolific work and continues to inspire me greatly to this day.

One of Jay's routines involves three balls of wool. He would juggle them as they unravelled and gradually entangled him. I loved this routine, and it would be so fitting for *K is for Knitting Club*. I asked for Jay's permission to use the idea ahead of the show and he very kindly said yes.

I performed the routine whilst walking around the audience and climbing over them. This was the perfect finale of the show because it tangled the entire audience up in wool, and bound them together.

After enough digging, one could probably find a meaningful metaphor in there somewhere about the wool-bound audience representing my show bringing people together, and that juggling plus comedy plus knitting equals oneness. The people are bound by the very materials they use to create. They are trapped in a loop of their own creativity. Either way, the audience was happy and it was a joy to see.

Juggling with wool – and tangling up an audience of knitters in the process – was one of those unique experiences I never would have had if I hadn't embarked on this tour.

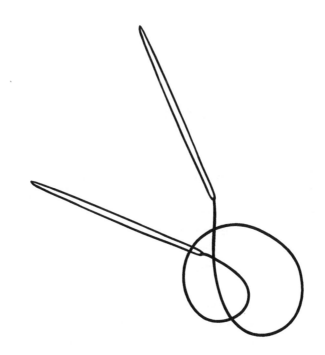

L IS FOR LIBRARY

Like a knife through butter, we were now gliding through The ABC Tour with ease. The previous two shows had been a success and were a lot of fun to perform. It felt like we were about to have a lot more like this in the pipeline. At almost the halfway point, I felt that it was going to be onwards and upwards, from here on out.

I like books and I own way more than I'll ever get around to reading. As well as offering remarkably focused insights into authors' minds, I love that they can fill nooks and crannies of houses and, in a way, can be used as decoration.

A book collection offers a snapshot into the life of its owner: a cross-section of their tastes, influences and interests. I like going into people's houses (usually with their permission) and browsing their mini library. You can tell a lot about someone from the books they put on display.

I love the smell of a new book, fresh from the shop. I love the smell of an old book that's been sitting collecting dust. This also explains why, for 'L', I was drawn to performing at a library. There were many other choices, and some of the ones I rejected were, in all honesty, better options than a library:

Lavatory
I love the idea of going into a bar and saying, "Juggling and comedy show happening in the toilets in 10 minutes!". Then I'd go and get ready in a cubicle, and perform my show to the drunk and confused folks who stumbled in. I eventually decided against this, as filming would be tricky due to privacy concerns. Also, I had the option to revive this idea as *T is for Toilet* if I changed my mind.

Laboratory
This would be great too. I could have mixed juggling with some kind of science experiment or chemical reaction. I don't know

any science experiments or chemical reactions, or laboratories, or scientists. Apart from that, this was a solid option.

Laundrette
Visually, doing a show in front of the large washing machines would look quite hip, and I could finish the show by putting my props in the machine. A great option.

Lingerie Shop
An almost perfect suggestion. If I wasn't so set on a library, I could even let it slide that this is technically *S is for Shop*.

Lighthouse
I really like this. At the time of writing, I am thirty-two years old and I have never been in a lighthouse. Hopefully this sad state of affairs has changed by the time you are reading this sentence. The problem with lighthouses – and this is coming from someone who has never been in one – is that I suspect it doesn't look like a lighthouse when you are inside. Therefore, it wouldn't be great for filming.

Lake or Lagoon
Still one of my biggest regrets about the tour is that I didn't perform in water. I could have done lake, lagoon, weir, river, stream, swimming pool, bath, puddle, sea, ocean, fjord, and many other options, but I didn't. I'll save that for the "Jon Udry Braves the Elements" Tour.

Limo
I would have loved to hire a limo, drive around town and ask random members of the public to jump in for a juggling show. However, this could come across as a bit creepy. Only a fool would entice strangers into a vehicle for a show.

Even though a lot of these ideas were great, as I said, I like books – and I was drawn to performing in a library. My first choice was the largest library in my home city, Bristol Central Library. It was split into two levels: the ground floor had low ceilings, carpeted floors and aisles of bookshelves that you could weave through and look over the top, like a hedge maze, while upstairs was completely different. It had floor-to-ceiling bookshelves, ornate spiral staircases leading up to mezzanines, dark wooden floors, high ceilings, large wooden desks and antique books. It looked like the type of library you'd find at Hogwarts.

This is where I wanted to do my show. In all honesty, I thought I was punching above my weight with this venue but I needed to aim high.

A few days after speaking to the manager, Polly, I entered the library's mundane ground floor to meet with her. From the get-go, she seemed excited and intrigued about this ridiculous project. I had expected that she'd grant us permission to do a show on the ground floor but I didn't expect what happened next. Polly took us upstairs to the grand, necromantic first floor library. We wandered around on our private tour and discussed potential show locations. Then, after a brief tête-à-tête, Polly granted me permission to do a show in the magical library. ALAKAZAM!

On the day of the show I was joined by Anton, Courtney and Dan, who were helping out. We unloaded The ABC Tour bus (aka my VW Golf) and started setting up. Polly and the staff were extremely helpful and totally up for doing whatever they could to make the show run smoothly. With their help, we moved the large wooden desks from one side of the room to the other to create a cavernous open performance space, framed by a backdrop of books.

Once we had set up the lights, sound, props and seats we were ready to go. It looked beautiful. I mean, really beautiful. This place was by far the most stunning set of The ABC Tour so far, even more so than the Aquarium. I loved how the lights created shadows that danced over the books and elongated into the high ceilings. If I dare say so myself, it even looked professional, which is lucky, because that is exactly what we were pretending to be.

Just before the audience arrived, Anton came up with one of his patented Good Ideas™. This was lucky, as Anton used to have the incredibly annoying habit of coming up with good ideas for ABC Tour shows about an hour after they had finished. It was morale-squashing and I eventually banned him from doing it.

The Good Idea™ was as follows: as the audience arrived, Anton would greet them at the door. He would ask them to say any word, and encouraged them to be as imaginative as possible. He would then write these words down on a list, give them a party popper, and explain to them that whenever their word was said during the show, they had to let their party popper off. This meant that, as well as doing a one hour show – of which fifteen minutes of it was brand new material – I had to keep looking at the list and thinking of ways to crowbar in such words as "dinosaur", "lavender" and "pineapple". I loved the idea of party poppers being let off at random moments throughout the show, especially as it was in a library. The problem with this idea was that most of the audience forgot their words, which meant that I was saying some crazy out-of-context nonsense, and then pausing for the pop. The pop wouldn't arrive, and then I'd have to repeat phrases like: "Do you know that dinosaurs used to eat lavender to help with their digestive system and to make their poo smell nice, like pineapple? Anyone?". Unfortunately this idea flopped but I still really like it as a concept.

This show contained the most new material devised specifically for the venue, up until this point of the tour. One of these was a routine with one of my favourite juggling books, *Virtuosos of Juggling* by Karl-Heinz Ziethen. This contained a handful of throws, catches and flourishes using a book containing throws, catches and flourishes, and finished up with me spinning a ball on the corner of the hard cover.

My favourite new section was some stand-up about a book that I learnt to juggle from at the age of nine, called *The Complete Juggler* by Dave Finnigan. I told the story about how nine-year-old me went to the library to take *The Complete Juggler* out with my library card and then, whenever it was due for renewal, I would return it to the library before taking it out again. This went on for about a year, until I had managed to get through the whole book.

I also included some poems in this show, which felt right for the setting. One of my favourite comedians is Nick Helm. Whenever I go to see Nick Helm I am always excited, because I am never sure what he is going to do as his shows are rarely just straight stand-up. He might come out and sing a song, then do some poetry, physical theatre or audience participation. I would love to head down that road a little more in the future and this show at the library definitely confirmed my desire for taking my performances in this direction.

My other favourite part (after all, I can have as many favourite parts as I want) was performing the helium balloon routine. It had been a while since I'd performed it under such a high ceiling. The balloons ascended at such a smooth and silent pace, unaware of how they inconvenienced not only the routine, but the venue when we had to retrieve them at the end. It reminded me why I love performing it.

After the show, I did have a little panic about how I could get the balloon down from such a great height, without a shotgun to hand. As you'll recall, I have a system that usually works, but I've never had to get a balloon down from so high before, and I had assured Polly that we'd get it down as she was concerned that, if we didn't, the balloon would fall in the night and set the alarms off for the library. However, luck was on my side that day and the system that hasn't failed me yet pulled through. I can't say I wasn't sweating over it though.

After I performed *H is for Hairdresser's*, I decided that I needed to stop taking the path of least resistance with the remaining shows on The ABC Tour. Venue-wise, L is for Library was as far from a challenge as I could get. The stage was spacious, level and well lit and the venue's staff were incredibly helpful. Despite it being a breeze in that regard, I still feel like I very much challenged myself with the material that I performed. The show consisted of fifteen minutes of new material that was library-specific. This – alongside the party-pooping party popper idea – made the show one that I am very proud of.

M IS FOR MONKEY SANCTUARY

Miraculously, I'd made it almost halfway through The ABC Tour – but I still had plenty of hurdles yet to jump. Buoyed by the success of *L is for Library*, I decided it was time to revisit something I'd tried and failed to do earlier in the tour: performing for animals.

As well as helping me out on some of the shows on the tour, Courtney also helped to book some of the venues. *M is for Monkey Sanctuary* was one of those venues. I was adamant that I wanted to do a show at a monkey sanctuary and so she duly called up Wild Futures – a monkey sanctuary in Looe, Cornwall – and sweet-talked them into hosting a performance. I was thrilled to hear that Courtney had managed to book a date for *M is for Monkey Sanctuary*, a matter of days after we'd first discussed it.

I love monkeys… but then, who doesn't? I think people love monkeys because they see them as a hairier and sillier version of ourselves. Perhaps, deep down, we all wish we could be a little bit more like our hirsute, jocular chums.

Courtney did a great job at booking the venue; however, I do not think that I did a great job at choosing it. I have to flag up the fact that *M is for Monkey Sanctuary* is breaking my rules, as it should technically be *S is for Sanctuary*. Unless, I did *M is for Monkey* and attempted to perform a show in or on a monkey, but I imagine that would go against the ethics of the sanctuary.

Putting these issues aside, I only wanted to do a show at the Monkey Sanctuary because I liked the idea of doing a show for animals and, since the dog shelters didn't want me, maybe I'd have more luck entertaining the monkeys. Frustratingly, there were so many other great possibilities for 'M', that in all honesty, I feel a little disappointed that I decided so adamantly on a Monkey Sanctuary instead of mulling it over and considering other venues:

MOTORWAY

Noisy, dangerous and - worst of all - nowhere for the audience to park.

MORGUE

Too creepy, and the last thing I needed on this tour was a tough crowd.

MALL

Plenty of parking available but not hugely challenging. Besides, I had done shows in shopping centres before.

MUSEUM

I liked this one a lot. Performing under a dinosaur skeleton (or a blue whale) would be fantastic.

MOON

Wonderful thought but difficult to get to and slightly out of my budget.

MUD PIT

This was also a great shout. Performing while traipsing through thick, goopy mud would have been a real challenge.

MINEFIELD
These are the types of places people suggest to me. Sickening. What did I ever do to you?

MONGOOSE ENCLOSURE
Don't mongooses (mongeese?) kill snakes? No thanks. Again, was it something that I said?

MATERNITY WARD
I can't imagine a woman giving birth is going to want to see a show – and I'm not willing to risk the wrath of angry new parents.

MAGIC SHOP
Magic shops are creepy places. I would definitely prefer to perform in a morgue, given the choice..

MAZE
This was a strong contender. We might have had a few late arrivals, however.

MARKET
This one leans towards the beige side of the rainbow. It's too much like a regular street show, unfortunately.

Alas, I chose the Monkey Sanctuary because, you know… monkeys.

On the day of the show, I loaded the equipment into the car at the crack of dawn. I then went to pick up Courtney and Dan and commenced our three-hour drive from Bristol to Cornwall. Thanks to the early start, we arrived at the Monkey Sanctuary in Looe with plenty of time to suss out the venue, and were even treated to a private tour by Sarah Hanson, our trusty guide.

The sanctuary is amazing and, as well as there being plenty of funky monkeys, it commands a mesmerising view of the ocean. I'd highly recommend going there if you can, and suggest going on a nice sunny day. We, however, did not go on a nice sunny day. Rain hammered down in apocalyptic proportions, but nonetheless, it was still an enjoyable place to be.

The weather brought with it a big old sack of challenges. As it was inclement turning horrid, the park didn't have the packed-out Easter weekend audiences that it expected. This meant that the visitors that braved the sodden sanctuary would have to have been very keen on the show. Unfortunately, the designated performance area was meant to

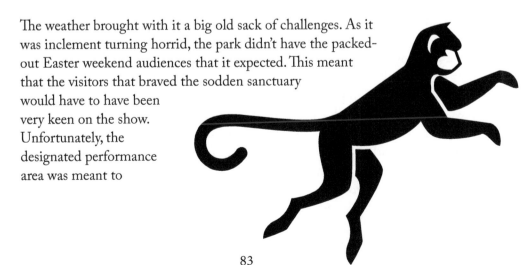

be outside. Sarah helpfully
presented to us an
alternative: a very
small marquee with
a raked stage and
comically low ceilings.

As the audience was
crammed in and sheltered
from the rain, this venue brought
with it a certain type of intimacy
that I hadn't experienced so far
on The ABC Tour. In *J is for Jail*,
the enclosed space was claustrophobic
and uncomfortable but here it was cosy and
warm. It also felt like we were bunched together sheltering from the rain; all
trying to survive this frankly awkward situation of doing a show in such tricky
circumstances.

The show itself, consisted of my standard material with balls and clubs, except
that I performed it in a squat position in order to gain more height for the
throws. The only exciting part of the show worth mentioning was an ad-lib
musical tube section with improvised juggling. Next to the stage, there was a
rack of plumbing pipes at a 45° angle, each cut to varying lengths. These were
here for people to use by hitting the opening of the tube with table tennis
paddles, and creating musical notes.

As they were there, it would have been a shame not to use them, so I brought
a child up to perform on the musical tubes whilst I improvised a juggling
routine. It really was a lot of fun. No doubt, with this leg up into show business,
the child has now gone on to record a number-one album of musical-tube
classics and will be headlining the Pyramid Stage of Glastonbury festival within
a few years. Probably.

After the show, I really wanted to have a crack at performing to the monkeys.
This idea basically stems from when I saw a YouTube video of someone doing
magic tricks for a chimpanzee: the furry fella completely lost his bananas when
the coin vanished from the magic man's hands. I am fully aware that a chimp is
an ape, rather than a monkey, but still, I wanted to see how they'd react to the
juggling. As it turned out, not only did the monkeys not like rain, they weren't
that keen on juggling either.

After having my ego damaged by the monkey snub, Dan, Courtney and I
were all adamant that we needed some footage of me performing to monkeys

one way or another. Sitting in the cafe, we noticed a shelf full of cuddly toy monkeys and had a shared eureka moment. We set all of the toys up on the table as a willing captive audience. I then performed some juggling, whilst Dan filmed from behind the toys, and Courtney was crouched down underneath the table puppeteering them. We were clutching at straws at this point but it was the best we could do.

Despite the weather, I think the show went down a treat. In all honesty, I think the rain helped. Without it, maybe the audience would've been more into the monkeys than my show. Maybe they would've had less focus. Without the rain, I wouldn't have had the opportunity to perform in such a tiny, intimate space. If it had been sunny, maybe the monkeys would've loved juggling so much that they would learn to master the craft and put me out of a job? I guess we will never know.

N IS FOR NATURIST RESORT

N ow that I had finally crossed the halfway mark of the tour, I was struck with a feeling that I might actually make it to the end and that there was no turning back. I could see the bright light at the end of the tunnel and, as it drew closer, it felt thrilling.

Of the shows that I had done thus far, some had been mentally challenging and there was definitely a moment when I really hadn't wanted to keep going with The ABC Tour. With the midway point now reached, I felt a sense of pride that I had made it this far and was pumped to get my teeth stuck into the next thirteen shows.

I have a problem with superfluous nudity in a theatrical setting – specifically in comedy and circus. I teach at a couple of circus schools in the UK: a pet peeve of mine is when students are creating new material and, as an attempt at delivering the "shock factor", decide to perform the material naked.

This trend is also seen in modern circus and cabaret a lot, where people will strip down to their pants and do their utmost to provoke the audience in a comical fashion. This doesn't make any sense to me.

A message to circus students: no one is shocked when you get naked for no reason on stage. Embarrassed, yes. Confused, yes. Ashamed, quite possibly. But shocked, no. Nudity for the sake of spectacle misses the mark.

To clarify, I am vehemently against nudity out of context on stage. However, make no mistake, I am not against nudity. I am not against being nude. I am not against being nude on stage. There just needs to be a valid context. This brings me to the next show on The ABC Tour: N is for Naturist Resort. If there was ever a context for performing naked, this was it. There were, of course, other suggestions for 'N' such as nail salon, nursery, nursing home or nightclub, but to be honest, none of them came close to the absurdity of performing at a Naturist Resort.

Courtney did some digging and found a naturist resort in St Albans called Spielplatz. Founded in 1929, Spielplatz is the longest-running naturist resort in the United Kingdom and, with its communal gardens, tennis courts, sun loungers and even an outdoor Jacuzzi, it remains very popular to this day. After what I can only assume was a combination of email magic, NLP and sheer charm, Courtney informed me that they'd be very keen to go ahead with the show.

On the day of the gig, because of the worries that were floating around my head, Courtney, Dan, Anton and I made the three-hour drive to Spielplatz feel like a six-hour drive. I was very nervous. In fact, more nervous than I had been at any point on The ABC Tour to date. My brain was inundated with all sorts of concerns and I was second-guessing everything.

What material should I do? Could I do it naked? Do I make a big deal out of the nakedness? Do I ignore it and treat it as a perfectly normal state out of respect for the naturists? Do I keep my shoes on? Where do I look? Do I use audience participation? Will people turn up? I also really hoped there was a high ceiling.

Driving along the path that led to the resort felt a little bit like we were driving through a safari park. Instead of looking out of the windows for monkeys, lions or giraffes, we were trying to spot the naturists through the cracks in the bushes, and the bushes through the cracks.

The venue itself was a carpeted, low-ceilinged clubhouse. A great place for a show, to be honest, except for the ceilings. Why did this have to be the show that had low ceilings? A low ceiling means more objects hitting the ceiling, which means more drops, which means more bending over. I was concerned enough about the show as it was without further impediments.

Moments later we were greeted by naturist, David Piper, who was serving as our contact for the venue. He was fully clothed at this point, which I hadn't realised was an acceptable practice in such a place. I spoke to him about my concerns with being naked for the show.

Normally, when I change into my suit for shows, it feels like I turn into a different kind of "me". A more amped up, confident and fearless version of Jon Udry. Wearing the suit gives me the ability to feel like I can do anything on stage. It makes me feel invincible.

One of my fears was that if I didn't have the suit on and I just wandered out onto a stage naked, in front of a naked audience, I would struggle to fabricate the faux confidence that the magical suit provides me with. Without the suit, maybe I was "vincible" after all.

It was 4pm and the show started at 8pm. David suggested that it was probably best if we got naked now, so that by the time the show came around, we would feel comfortable and would have forgotten that we were naked[13]. I gingerly started to strip off in front of my friends. This was incredibly awkward for everyone present, except for maybe David. I assume that, for him, his birthday suit has the same effect on him as my actual suit has on me. Like real troopers, Courtney and Dan joined me in disrobing. Anton, however, remained clothed as he has four extra nipples that he doesn't want anybody to know about.

David suggested that we hit the outdoor jacuzzi as a way of getting acclimatised to the naturist lifestyle. Feeling self-conscious, we slipped into the hot tub where, all of a sudden, things actually felt less tense. Yes, I was sitting naked in a big bath with my friends, but the fact that water was covering our bits and bobbins made it feel like we were un-naked.

---

[13] *It is worth mentioning that I was naked from 4:00pm until 9:30pm and at no point did I feel comfortable or forget I was naked.*

Occasionally, the feet of two different people would touch beneath the water's surface and it would be met with a very sheepish and British "Sorry!". It felt more inappropriate to touch a foot in the hot tub when you knew that the Netherlands were only a leg's stretch away.

On a side note, I don't care if you are an athlete, a supermodel or Miss Universe – everybody looks ridiculous getting in and out of a hot tub while naked.

After clumsily lugging our sodden selves out of the jacuzzi, we toweled off and started to get ready for the show. Courtney got changed back into her clothes, while Dan and myself remained *au naturel* for the rest of the evening.

As Dan was filming, he really had no need to be naked. To this day, I still have no idea why he remained starkers for the whole time, except for curiosity and moral support. In any event, it was very much appreciated as I didn't like the idea of being the only naked member of The ABC Tour team in the room.

Whilst we were taking a break from setting up the show, David came in to see how we were getting on. We sat down, naked as a pair of mole rats, and started talking about the evening's events.

David:
We are all very much looking forward to
tonight's show.

Me:
That's great. Me too. Am I right in saying
that you have had other performers do
shows here as well?

David:
Oh yes. We've had comedians, magicians,
singers, bands, all sorts...

Me:
Wow. And they all perform naked too?

David (shocked):
OH NO! Nobody performs naked. We
didn't think you were going to be doing the
show naked to be honest, but we're thrilled
to know that you are.

This wasn't the news I wanted to hear. With only a few hours
left until showtime, wearing nothing but a skittish smile, I had
just found out that it wasn't the norm to be doing a show naked
in a place where it's normal for people to be naked. My chest
tightened and my skittish smile got a bit more skittish.

With only moments until showtime, the stage, lights and
sound were set and I was ready in costume. In fact, this
particular costume I'd been wearing my entire life, so it hadn't
taken me any time to put on. The only two nudies in the room
at this point were myself and Dan.

The door at the back of the room opened and the naturists
entered. We were excited to meet our audience for the show but,
as they entered, we noticed something odd. Something quite
alarming. The naturists were here. Great. We had an audience.
Great. I was prepared to do a show naked. Fine. Dan was still
naked. Who knows why? Meanwhile, the naturists were fully
clothed.

Here we were, like a chilly pair of sphynx cats, at a naturist
resort, surrounded by naturists, but the two non-naturists were
the only ones starkers. At this point I was convinced that I'd
made a massive mistake but, one by one, the audience also
stripped off, hung up their clothes on hangers by the door, and
made their way to the seats. The ludicrousness of performing
naked was really starting to loom in, but hey, at least it was good
exposure[14].

---

[14] *This is Anton's joke. Direct any complaints his way.*

Moments before the show started, I was extremely nervous and developed a temporary eye twitch to join my tight chest. They say that when you are nervous in front of a crowd, you should imagine them all naked.

In this case, no imagination was needed. I introduced myself from behind a screen, then walked out, barefoot and bare-bodied, onto the stage and stood before my naked crowd in all my glory.

Sometimes, when I perform on big stages the lights are so bright that I can't see the faces of the audience. I prefer this; I tend to get more nervous when I can see their faces. However, in this case, I could see their faces, and everything else, which really didn't help.

Conversely, I have a recurring nightmare where I am backstage at a theatre. I hear my name being introduced but I am not quite ready. Regardless, I run out on stage to do my show but then, after a minute or so, I look down and realise I have no trousers on. Experts in dream analysis, get in touch to tell me what this means.

My nightmare became a reality when this time I looked down, not only did I not have any trousers on, but also no underwear, or socks, or shoes, or shirt, or anything. This was worse than my recurring nightmare – but it was real.

Obviously, I knew the structure of the show I planned to perform, but as I hadn't performed the show naked before, I was almost figuring it out as I went. I'll tell you something for nothing – when you are juggling naked, there is a surprising amount of wiggling and waggling. It's really quite distracting to have the flipping and flopping whilst jiggling and juggling. It's more than you can imagine. I like to think that, at this point, you are either imagining yourself juggling naked, or you are imagining me juggling naked. Win-win.

The stage area was carpeted, which made everything that bit more challenging. I tend to move around quite a lot during my performances and the soles of my feet were soon covered in carpet burns.

Sometimes during shows I'll use a microphone attached to my face with a headband. This frees up my hands to do the business that they need to do, which makes the performance a lot easier.

For this gig, I couldn't use a head mic, as I didn't have any pockets to put the receiver in; additionally, any alternatives to pockets didn't seem particularly appealing. As a compromise, I used a classic handheld microphone with a lead, on a mic stand. When talking, I would walk around with the microphone and every now and then; as I did this, a surprising sensation occurred that I had never felt before. The mic lead would clip the end of my chap, which would throw me off and surprise me every time. So much so that I had to tell the audience about it. I didn't hate it, if I'm honest.

After the show, I was invited to have a beer with the audience at the bar at the back of the room. One of the audience members was actually the barmaid, so she very kindly poured me a pint.

I stood there naked, with my naked audience (and, of course, naked Dan), having a pint, whilst making way more eye contact than I normally would in a clothed bar. Despite how nervous I was, the whole thing really was a delightful experience. I have to say though, I thoroughly enjoyed popping my clothes back on once it was all over.

Photos: Courtney Propokas

O IS FOR ORIGAMI CONVENTION

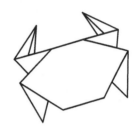

O n the face of it, finding a suitable venue for 'O' should have been easy, as there are an abundance of words that begin with it. However, despite my best efforts (and those of the social media researchers), I really found it tough to find something that was interesting – and feasible – enough for The ABC Tour.

OIL RIG

Initially, this seems like a great idea. However, an oil rig only looks like one when you're not on it – so it's unfortunately a no from me.

OFFICE

This feels like the kind of place I would have chosen at the start of the tour when I was just trying to cross off letters. A boring choice.

ORANGERY

I honestly thought an orangery was a place that grew oranges. As it turns out to be another word for conservatory, it's a bit dull.

ORGY

Too distracting. Besides, I'd seen more than enough naked flesh for one juggling tour.

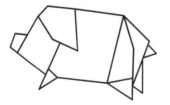

OPERA

I've performed in operas before – and a 3 min cameo in 'The Bartered Bride' isn't really in the ABC Tour spirit.

OBSERVATORY

It was an option – but I just found it a bit on the boring side. A place designed for looking out, when I wanted people looking in.

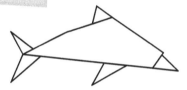

I eventually settled on *O is for Origami Convention*. I had already broken five rules up to this point, and I didn't feel great about breaking another. *D is for Door Shop* (*S is for Shop*), *E is for Eden Project* (*B is for Biome*), *K is for Knitting Club* (*C is for Club*), *M is for Monkey Sanctuary* (*S is for Sanctuary*), *N is for Naturist Resort* (*R is for Resort*) and now here I was, breaking the rules a sixth time with *O is for Origami Convention* (*C is for Convention*). However, this tour was far from ordinary, and a certain amount of chaos was to be expected. *C is for Chaotic Tour* (*T is for Tour*).

After some research we discovered that, in a few months, the British Origami Society (BOS) would be holding a convention in Colchester, southeast England. Better yet,

Courtney worked her emailing charm and managed to get me booked to perform a show at the end of the convention.

Conveniently, I was already booked to perform at the British Juggling Convention (BJC) in Canterbury (approximately 100 miles from Colchester) the day before *O is for Origami Convention*. With *N is for Naturist Resort* also scheduled a couple of days before the BJC, we had ourselves a little ABC Tour road trip.

The BJC is a large annual event held over a few days, featuring multiple workshops, competitions, shows, many vendors selling all sorts of juggling paraphernalia, a 24-hour juggling practice space, and more jugglers than you can shake a stick at.

That year it was held in Canterbury and I was booked to perform in the main gala show, which took place in the magnificent Margate Winter Gardens.

Jugglers are nerds. I mean no disrespect when I say that. I'm sure that you probably think I'm a hella cool cat, but deep down, I'm a nerdboy. To be honest, I think in order to be a juggler, you have to be a touch on the nerdy side. I think that any able-bodied person can learn to juggle, but I don't think that anyone can learn to be a juggler. You need to be obsessed with the intricacies of the art form and find joy in the journey of constant failure. You need to relish in spending hundreds, if not thousands of hours picking things up off the floor, by yourself. It's this environment that nerds and dweebs, like myself, blossom in.

It turns out that a similar personality type is drawn towards origami. Prior to the convention, I put a post out on social media saying that I was going to be attending the BJC and that, if anyone knew how to make any origami, they should come and find me as I would love to use it as decoration in my upcoming show, *O is for Origami Convention.*

As soon as I arrived at the BJC, I was welcomed with boxes and bags of various origami sculptures, everything from the classic crane to an intricate, tiny Yoda. We now had everything we needed to decorate the room for *O is for Origami Convention.* You can always rely on the nerds.

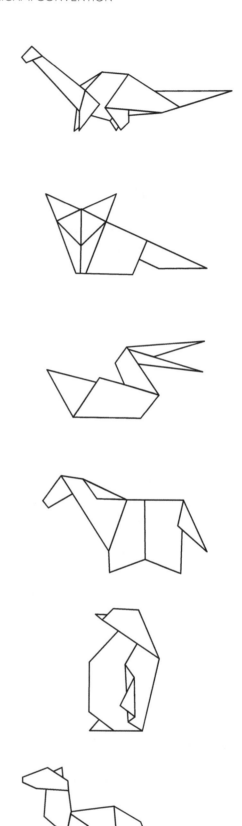

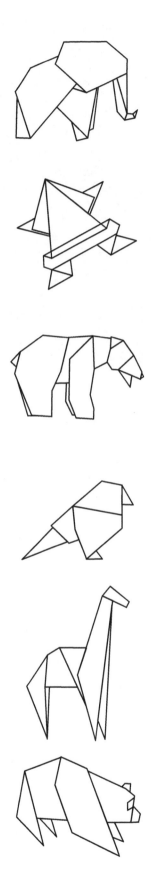

Quite naively, I assumed that the British Origami Convention would be the same, if not bigger than the BJC. I was anticipating workshops of various paper-folding techniques, a stationery shop, a 24-hour origami dojo, speed folding competitions, a massive origami crane, and more origamians than you can shake a sheet of kami at.

Once again, as I had been so often on this tour, I was dead wrong. We walked into the building where the convention was being held and had the feeling that perhaps we were in the wrong place or that we'd arrived on entirely the wrong day.

With a juggling convention, you can typically tell where it is being held from about a mile away, as there will be a hippy riding a unicycle as if it were a normal means of transport, or someone wearing a floppy clown juggling hat as if it were an ordinary piece of clothing.

Here at the British Origami Convention, there were no such sights. We had to look hard for any signs of paper folding at all! Not only did it feel like we were at the wrong venue, it didn't even feel like the building was open. We walked through its ghostly corridors trying to find any signs of life (or folded paper).

We finally found our contact for the day, Adam, who took us to the room where I was going to be doing the show. It felt like a school classroom, with one of its walls being an entire blackboard. Come to think of it, perhaps it was a classroom. Either way, it was a blank canvas for us and we had one hour to transform

this room into what looked like an origami show. I started to sketch out a plan on the table, until Courtney rightfully pointed out that, instead of doing a plan on the table about the room that we were in, we could just use the room that we were in to make the plan. She's a smart cookie.

We found some large chalk, so I got on the case with drawing The ABC Tour backdrop of the stage on the large chalkboard. I felt like Neil Buchanan from *Art Attack*.

Whilst I was doing this, Courtney and Anton crisscrossed string above the stage, and then hung the plethora of origami, donated by the jugglers, onto it. I have to say, this, with the backdrop and the lights, really did look very beautiful. In my opinion, this was the best-looking stage setting so far on the tour.

Along came showtime. The origamish people turned up and, considering this was a free show as part of their annual convention, fewer attended than I'd expected. I know that juggling isn't for everyone but a part of me thought that, as I had found out that a lot of jugglers are into origami, I assumed the passion would be reciprocated. I was wrong again. They clapped, they wearily cheered, they made an effort but, in all honesty, I don't think they liked the show that much.

My material received a lukewarm response and many of my jokes failed to land; all-in-all, it felt like an incredibly slow hour.

I don't blame them: I can't please everybody. I had assumed that the nerdiness of jugglers would be the same as the nerdiness of origamists, but I was wrong. They are on another level. To be clear: not necessarily a higher level, just a different level.

At the end of the show, my heart was in my stomach. A man from the audience came up to me and looked me dead in the eyes. I expected the worst but instead he said, "You're a star". He then gently grabbed me by the wrist, and with his other hand placed a £20 note (the second cash payment of the tour) folded into the shape of a star into my hand.

It was as uncomfortable as it sounds but the gesture was very sweet. Maybe the audience didn't hate me as much as I thought. It certainly wouldn't be the first time I had thought I performed a bad show and then later found out from people that they loved it. Classic performer insecurities.

A few minutes passed, and a woman from the audience came up to me and looked me dead in the eyes, and said, "You're a star" with quite cultish similarities to the first man. She then grabbed my wrist, and with the other hand placed a piece of paper folded up into the shape of a star, into my hand. An identical star to the £20 note star that I now had in my pocket, except hers was just an ordinary piece of paper.

I did the right thing. I took the £20 star out of my pocket and secretly concealed it in my hand. I showed her the star of paper that she had just given me, and then I said – in a very David Blaine manner – "Watch closely". I rubbed my hands together, switching the cheap

star for the money star without her noticing. She witnessed the miracle of my turning her paper star into a £20 note star. She lost her mind and ran out of the room as if she had just witnessed real magic.

I guess where I had gone wrong was in expecting the origamayans to be exactly the same as jugglers, when in fact our passions are totally different. When someone juggles, the experience is over as soon as the last object is caught… but with origami, the art form endures until the sculpture ceases to exist.

This left me wondering: if someone gave me a piece of origami, what should I do with it? Am I meant to keep it forever? Do I stick it to my fridge? Could I put it in the bin? Is that rude? It's mine now, so surely I can do whatever I want with it. Right? Or wrong? I don't know.

I was left with the predicament of now owning an entire box of beautifully folded origami sculptures kindly donated to me by the loving jugglers of my community. I love jugglers. But I wasn't too keen on owning a box of stuff I didn't want to have.

This left me with only one option. I set it all on fire. It felt good.

P IS FOR PIGPEN

Previously on The ABC Tour, I'd not had much luck with non-human audiences. First off, I'd failed in my attempt to perform for dogs. Then I'd struggled to get the monkeys interested in watching me juggle in the rain. So far, it had been a rough tour with my animal buddies, but I thought I'd give it another crack and try my hand at performing for my squeelin', wheelin', rollin'-in-dung dealin' friends: the pigs. Ideally, I wanted to perform inside an actual pig pen, although I was aware that this was a bit of a long shot.

I love animals. A lot of the time, I love them more than humans. Dogs, monkeys, pigs: I love them all and always have. Except for bats. I don't have any time for bats. I don't like their little faces or the way that they never fly in a straight line. They take the longest route that squanders the most energy, to get from A to B. How can you trust an animal that makes those kinds of decisions? They are blind yet they always fly at night? Oh please! How do they know? Chuck in the fact that they sleep upside down, drink blood and have no reflection. Keep them away from me, thank you very much. However, all other animals are great.

At the age of four, I owned a worn leather satchel of plastic animals that my parents had picked up from a car-boot sale. Every time we'd go to one of these sales, which was a regular occurrence, I would keep my eyes peeled for more animals and, if I was lucky and on my best behaviour, my parents might buy them for me to add to my made-up menagerie. These animals would be locked up in leather-bound captivity until they were daily reintroduced into the wilderness of the living room, where they would roam the plains of the 1980's carpet.

One game I often played was to line the 300 or so animals up in single file around the house. I would meticulously place them on their feet, hooves, paws, hands, claws, trotters or stomachs, one in front of the other. If anyone walked too close to the animal queue, their footsteps risked toppling a tiger, jolting a giraffe, or collapsing a camel. If the felling of such fauna would occur, I would lose my rag and scream the heavens down in anger. Justifiably so, I think. I can't keep my elephants on their feet, if people are traipsing around on their own feet, like elephants. Considering my youthful preoccupation with structure and order, it came as no surprise that the moment I discovered juggling, I quickly became utterly obsessed by it. Juggling can only exist with structure and order.

I'd heard from some entertainers in the industry that there was a place in Devon, called Pennywell Farm, that had a very hands-on approach to people visiting the farm animals and, in particular, the pigs. A lot of entertainers tend to do shows here throughout the tourist season and, without trying to dwell on the fact that I had never been booked for this gig that so many of my colleagues seemed to know so well, I started looking into it.

Typically, the booked performers do their shows in an amphitheatre set up in a barn, with lights and sound rigged up. Normally I'd really like this sort of gig (If you are reading this, Pennywell Farm, I would still like this gig. I live in Bristol. It's not far away). Yet, as you'll know by now, this was the opposite of my vision for The ABC Tour. When I went to the farm, I noticed that a lot of visitors were cuddling pigs. This place seemed to have such lax rules with regards to their animals, rules that couldn't be further away from those of *M is for Monkey Sanctuary*.

Valerie Bickford-Beers, the manager of the farm, was so onboard with the idea that we set a date for *P is for Pig Pen* right there and then. As we were walking around the farm, some suggestions were thrown at me as to where I might perform the show. Firstly, she showed me the barn amphitheatre. You know the one – the

one that every South-West England entertainer has performed in except for me. Making my best efforts to rise above this, I told her that it wasn't really what I was looking for and that I wanted to get more involved with the animals.

I was then taken to a pig pen, which held about a dozen miniature pigs. I'm sure that at least one person reading this will be thinking, *surely he means piglets?* – and no, I don't. These are fully grown adult pigs, though no bigger than a chubby Chihuahua. With my previous experience from the monkey sanctuary, I assumed Valarie would suggest that I could perform outside the pen, to the pigs, with the human audience watching from the other side. How wrong I was.

Valerie:
So here's the pig pen.

Me:
It looks great.

Valerie:
Well, do you want to try it out?

Me:
What do you mean? I have never tried out a pig pen before.

Valerie:
Pop in and try it out. See if you can do your show in there.

I ungracefully climbed over the fence like a grandparent getting out of a bunk bed, trying my best not to trample on any of the excitable little swines that were keen to meet their new visitor. I walked amongst the pigs, swishing my feet through the hay and faecal matter, took a quick look up to check the ceiling height, and replied...

Me:

Yeah. This'll be perfect! But obviously there won't be the pigs in here whilst I do the show, right?

Valerie:

They will be if you want them to be. If there are no pigs in the pig pen, it's just a pen, isn't it?

Me:

You've got a point.

Valerie:

Just don't drop anything on them.

Before I left, we took a few photos so we could use them to promote the show. The next time I'd return would be the day of the show.

A few weeks later, we arrived at the farm to perform. I was excited, but more than a little anxious. Obviously, I had never performed a show in a space surrounded by live animals before. I didn't really know what to expect, or even what to do. As ever, I donned my three-piece suit, this time accessorised with a pair of elegant green wellies (for those of you outside of the UK, these are unflattering, knee-high, waterproof boots), and before I knew it, it was show time.

I clambered into the pig pen, and quite predictably, the pigs became very excited. Presumably, because they thought I was bringing them food. That and the fact that I was wearing a suit, may have caused them to think it was a special occasion where I might be serving truffles, pancakes or lasagne. Not today, tiny, little, hungry hogs! This chef was bringing a three-course meal of juggling, comedy and nonsense. Sorry!

After positioning myself in the centre of the pen and explaining
to the bemused audience on the other side of the fence what the
Duke of Heckington was going on, I began the show. My first
trick was to bounce a ball on my head whilst making a balloon dog
behind my back. It turns out that the pigs were particularly into
this trick, so(w) much so(w) that they were soon trying to climb my
legs to get a closer look.

Needless to say, this made it a lot trickier as I couldn't move
my feet without fear of trodding on a trotter. During this trick I
typically talk to the audience and crack a couple of jokes. However,
the excited pigs meant that the noise of the oinks, squeals and
grunts rendered me inaudible. I had completely underestimated the
sheer volume that a dozen pigs could produce – a valuable lesson
for when you next find yourself doing a comedy juggling show in a
pig pen.

Accepting that talking was now out of the question, I decided to do
a bounce juggling routine specifically for the pigs. On my previous
visit to the farm, I noticed that beneath the hay, the floor of the
pen was a smooth concrete surface. If the words "smooth concrete
surface" don't make you hot under the collar, then you are not a
bounce juggler. Other than polished granite or marble, it is one of
the best surfaces for bouncing balls off of.

I began my routine, moving around the pen making sure to
bounce the balls off the floor where the pigs weren't. A lot trickier
than it sounds, as the pigs seemed to be very intrigued, not about
the juggling itself, but more likely as to why the juggling was
happening, and wondering when they might next snaffle a tasty
piece of fruit.

My routine approached the section where I lie down on the floor
and start to juggle through my legs. During this, I had pigs sniffing
my face, climbing over my legs, arms, and torso. I looked like I was
wearing a Lady Gaga garment. As I lifted my legs up to juggle
through them, a pig took notice of my pert peaches, and decided to
have a little taste of what was on offer. Right then, I feel the curious

teeth of a starving sow sink into my buttcheeks. I quickly stood up and carried on with the routine but I swear that when I looked down to see the biting swine, I saw her crack(l)ing up. That was the first, and hopefully the last, time I have been bitten in the buttock by a pig.

Up until this point of the show, I wasn't sure if the pigs were that into the juggling act. I don't think they hated it; I just feel that, as soon as they realised I wasn't giving them food, they found it a bit bo(a)ring. Understandably so. You could show me a group of naked dancers, juggling on a Caribbean beach, whilst I am sat on the sand with the sea lapping at my toes, getting a head massage from a world class masseuse and listening to Ben Folds Five, but, if I am hungry, I am not going to enjoy it.

    With this in mind, I changed tack and decided to give my porcine pals what they wanted. The farmer gave me some pig food in a bucket and, for some reason, gave me a wok to feed them from. I feel silly that I never even questioned the choice of a wok at the time. I poured some food into it and gradually sprinkled it around the pen whilst juggling using my other hand. To spice things up a little, I juggled all three objects, the wok of food and two juggling balls. This caused the pig food to be scattered all over the pen and, from their perspective, was probably the highlight of the show.

Other than some teeth marks on my bum, I came out unscathed. It was without a doubt the hardest show on The ABC Tour so far. Being surrounded by pigs and not being able to communicate to the audience properly made this a show that I'll never want to forget, and I genuinely cringe whenever I remember it. While it was a real struggle, I got through the performance and emerged if not stronger and better, certainly wise enough to not try juggling for pint-sized pigs again. This kind of show was exactly what The ABC Tour was meant to be about, so overall, you could call it a success. Just not one I'd want to repeat.

Q IS FOR QUIZ

Quite what I was thinking with this tour, I don't really know. At this point, it already felt like I'd been run through the mill: being shunned by monkeys, spending an awkward hour in a gallery, breathing in a face full of smoke in the forest, and being exposed to a constant stream of indecency on the internet; not to mention dog shelter rejection, naked uneasiness, and a pig biting me in the butt. And for what, exactly? It was quite late in the tour to be asking a question like this, as I was already approaching letter seventeen of the alphabet. It felt like some of my recent bad experiences had sightly soured the tour. Either that or it was just simply project-fatigue.

I knew that I couldn't just stop now and give up. I had ten shows left and there is no way that I wouldn't do them – that just wasn't an option. Little did I know just how challenging those final ten shows would prove to be.

After spinning the disaster that was *P is for Pig Pen* into a success story so I could stay positive, it was now time for 'Q'. After some online research, I found that only 1.56% of all English words begin with the letter 'Q' (which helps account for its obscene point-value in scrabble). Of this 1.56%, seldom of these words

were locations where I could perform a show on a ludicrous tour. Some of the meagre options included:

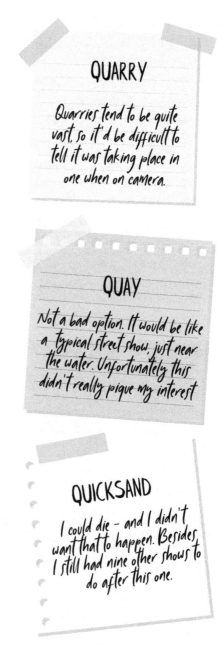

QUARRY

Quarries tend to be quite vast, so it'd be difficult to tell it was taking place in one when on camera.

QUAY

Not a bad option. It would be like a typical street show, just near the water. Unfortunately this didn't really pique my interest

QUICKSAND

I could die – and I didn't want that to happen. Besides, I still had nine other shows to do after this one.

QUARANTINE

Clearly this tour was ahead of its time. If only Covid had struck earlier then this could have been a convenient option.

However, as no one else could be there, it would need to be live streamed in which case this was a bit too similar to 'I is for Internet'.

QUEUE

When I started my career, I used to do these awful gigs where I'd juggle fire outside of nightclubs to entertain the chilly punters waiting to go inside and grind

all over one another. Having already done this and not enjoyed it one bit, I doubt I would have found it any more palatable two thirds of the way through a difficult tour like this.

As far as I could tell, this left me with no other option other than to do a quiz. Lucky enough, Marky Jay (who lent me the fire juggling clubs for *C is for Castle*), hosted a very popular pub quiz once a month in Bristol at a venue called The Canteen.

Better still, this was no ordinary quiz. Marky would follow the regular format of a pub quiz with questions and answers, but would also throw in rounds involving arts and crafts, mime, dance or whatever other activities he could think of that strayed from the path of the regular mundane quiz experience.

This unexpected jollification, mixed with Marky's showmanship and zest, added a levity to the quiz environment which helped make it a very popular evening. He kindly offered me his gig for one night, so I could perform *Q is for Quiz*. The issue now was: how could I host a quiz and somehow get away with calling it a show?

Firstly, I should point out that not only had I never hosted a quiz, but I had never even been on a team that had won a quiz. I am an extremely un-valuable quiz member and I feel sorry for any team that is burdened with me. I have no interest in any sports and my general knowledge is generally unknowledgeable. Unless there is a round about juggling history, animals or internet fail videos, then I am really just a sticky cog in what could otherwise be a well-oiled machine.

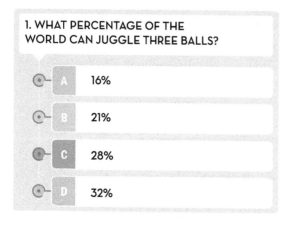

1. WHAT PERCENTAGE OF THE
WORLD CAN JUGGLE THREE BALLS?

A 16%

B 21%

C 28%

D 32%

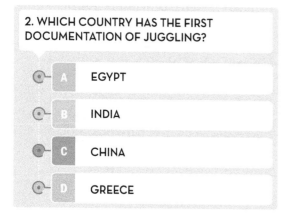

2. WHICH COUNTRY HAS THE FIRST
DOCUMENTATION OF JUGGLING?

A EGYPT

B INDIA

C CHINA

D GREECE

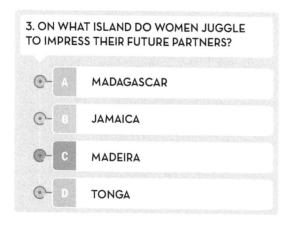

3. ON WHAT ISLAND DO WOMEN JUGGLE
TO IMPRESS THEIR FUTURE PARTNERS?

A MADAGASCAR

B JAMAICA

C MADEIRA

D TONGA

Undeterred, Anton, Courtney and I met up in the pub for a few tax-deductible pints so we could brainstorm ideas as to how I could successfully perform a fusion of juggling, comedy and quizzing. I wanted it to include the fun frivolities that Marky brought to the quiz but also wanted it to contain some juggling razzle-dazzle from my show. As Courtney had written quiz questions before, she was happy to take on the role of writing the questions, which was music to my ears.

We decided that I would perform some material and then ask people questions about what they had just seen, such as "how long was the track?", "which commercial made this track famous?" and "approximately how many throws and catches were in the routine?". After this, I would then ask some regular quiz type questions and follow it with some silly interactive shenanigans.

Personally, I think this format worked quite well, apart from the fact that we had massively over-prepared how much material we would need. The entire show and quiz went on for almost three hours, making it the longest show on The ABC Tour. Needless to say, this was too long and we finished the quiz with fewer teams than when we started.

Courtney did a great job at writing the questions, but I felt entirely out of place taking on the role of a serious quiz-master; especially as I had planned fun games and silly activities that were interspersed throughout the evening. It felt like I was wearing many different hats and only a couple of them were actually comfortable to put on.

It may come as no surprise that the parts of the evening I enjoyed the most were the puerile games; my highlight being a game that my good friend Arron Sparks and I invented many moons ago called "Bounce or No Bounce". I would take a random object such as a shoe, some chewing gum or a banana, and I would say to the audience, "Bounce or No Bounce?". They would then have to write down if they thought the object would bounce or not. I would then proceed to chuck it at the ground as hard as I could, with the full intention of making it bounce. It only counts if it bounces above knee level. It is a very fun game and if you haven't played it before – and statistically speaking, you haven't – then I cannot recommend it enough. You can play it anywhere too. Except for on a frozen lake. Or on a beach. Or on the Moon.

After the show I was exhausted and, quite honestly,

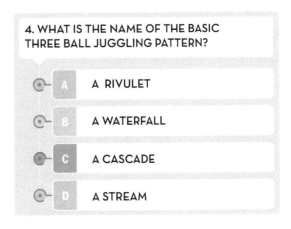

4. WHAT IS THE NAME OF THE BASIC THREE BALL JUGGLING PATTERN?

A   A RIVULET

B   A WATERFALL

C   A CASCADE

D   A STREAM

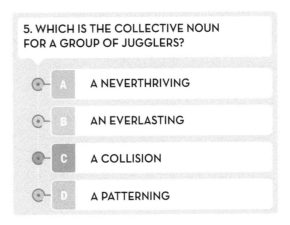

5. WHICH IS THE COLLECTIVE NOUN FOR A GROUP OF JUGGLERS?

A   A NEVERTHRIVING

B   AN EVERLASTING

C   A COLLISION

D   A PATTERNING

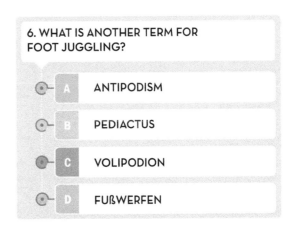

6. WHAT IS ANOTHER TERM FOR FOOT JUGGLING?

A   ANTIPODISM

B   PEDIACTUS

C   VOLIPODION

D   FUßWERFEN

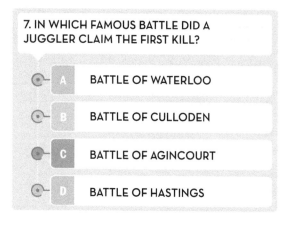

7. IN WHICH FAMOUS BATTLE DID A JUGGLER CLAIM THE FIRST KILL?

- A BATTLE OF WATERLOO
- B BATTLE OF CULLODEN
- C BATTLE OF AGINCOURT
- D BATTLE OF HASTINGS

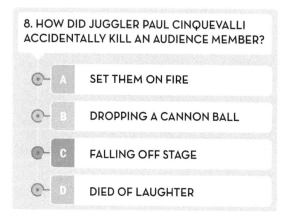

8. HOW DID JUGGLER PAUL CINQUEVALLI ACCIDENTALLY KILL AN AUDIENCE MEMBER?

- A SET THEM ON FIRE
- B DROPPING A CANNON BALL
- C FALLING OFF STAGE
- D DIED OF LAUGHTER

9. WHICH OBJECT WAS THE STANDARD SIZE OF JUGGLING RING MODELLED ON?

- A A FRISBEE
- B A BISCUIT TIN
- C A CHILD'S BIKE WHEEL
- D A DINNER PLATE

deflated. The quiz went fine: it wasn't great, but it was fine. I was left wishing I'd had another chance to do it because I would have changed so much about the night.

Firstly, it was too long. Secondly, as it was too long, people were getting tired and the serious quiz sections felt heavy (perhaps this was just my attitude as I know I am not a quizzer).

The fun parts, such as "Bounce or No Bounce" went down well but there just weren't enough of those moments. It felt like I had been trying to fit too many different activities into the same show.

One moment I was a solemn quiz-master, the next I was a comedy juggler and then – all of a sudden – I was a game show host. Flitting around these genres, instead of just focusing on one and making it as good as possible, was what squeezed the air out of my balloon that night.

I knew I could've done better. I went for quantity over quality and had no one else to blame but myself. Courtney's questions were great; I felt the game show bits worked well too. Also, the comedy and juggling breaks between the questions felt like breaths of fresh air throughout the quiz.

Despite that, the whole thing combined led to a mass mélange that I wasn't too pleased with.

At the end of the day, I did what I'd set out to do and performed a show that was also a quiz. It didn't matter if I enjoyed it at all. What mattered to me at that point was that I had ticked a rather tricky letter off the list. The end of the ABC Tour was in sight.

10. WHICH OF THESE IS NOT A TYPE OF JUGGLING CLUB?

- A RADICAL FISH
- B FAT HEAD
- C SPANKER
- D BEARD BEACH

Answers

1. B   2. A   3. D   4. C   5. A   6. A   7. D   8. C   9. B   10. C

R IS FOR ROLLER DISCO

Recovering from the ennui of *Q is for Quiz*, I knew that I had to crank the tour up a notch for the last nine letters of the alphabet. Annoyingly, for the letter 'R' we had an unusual predicament: for once, there were too many good options to choose from which made it quite tough to settle on a decision.

ROOF

The idea of performing on a roof felt like it'd be pretty rock and roll - like the Beatles' last performance in 1969 - except with no singing, more juggling and fewer fans.

RUBBISH DUMP

If I did this, the show could make use of items found at the rubbish dump that day. I love the idea - but it would be a health and safety nightmare.

RADIO

Courtney came up with this idea and at the time I wasn't sold on it. In retrospect, I'd like the challenge of making a juggling show specifically for radio[15]

---

[15] I have actually juggled on the radio twice in my life, which in my opinion is twice too many. The first time I was backstage at Glastonbury Festival, teaching BBC Radio One DJ Scott Mills how to juggle live on air. The other was shortly after I won British Young Juggler of the Year in 2005, which earned me a short-lived burst of press attention. Journalists from Radio 5 Live came to my school, entered my class, stopping the entire lesson for ten minutes whilst they interviewed me, surrounded by my shushed classmates. If this wasn't embarrassing enough, I was asked to juggle five balls for the duration of the interview while they asked me questions. I have no idea why they wanted this, as the pitter-patter of the balls as they slapped against my palms created what I thought was quite an annoying sound-bed for the interview. Besides, I could've just juggled three, and said it was seven! To this day, I still don't know why we didn't leave the classroom. It was a strange time.

As *I is for Ice Rink* was cancelled, I instead took the opportunity to try the land-based, four-wheeled sister of the ice skate: the roller skate. The plan was to learn how to do my entire show on roller skates and then take it to a roller disco. There were a few obstacles. Most pressingly, I'd actually need to learn to roller skate. How hard could it be?

It turns out that I took to roller skating just like Bambi took to being on ice. Slightly worse, in fact. I was not a natural, that's for sure. I knew I needed help, and so I called upon my good friend and multi-talented roller skating legend, Auntie Rick. Auntie Rick is the baddest (as in good-est) roller-skating Auntie in the region and they were adamant that, with a little bit of training, they'd be able to teach me to freak, crunk and groove, whilst hopefully not falling flat on my rump. During training, ironically my rump was the only part of my body not covered in protective wear. It's fair to say I was overly cautious in that regard.

The first thirty minutes of my training with Auntie Rick consisted of learning about what to do when you anticipate a fall. Normally, when you predict a tumble, the instinct is to flail around and try to regain your balance. Counterintuitively, this normally results in increasing your chances of falling. Auntie recommended that, when I was skating and felt like I might crumple on my rumple, I should bend my knees and lower myself to the ground in a ball. A similar approach to danger than that of a hedgehog or woodlouse. Have you ever seen a hedgehog or woodlouse fall over whilst skating? I rest my case.

After I was safe in the knowledge of knowing that the worst thing that would happen to me on skates would be to turn myself into a tripping hazard for other skaters, I felt quietly confident. With my training with Auntie complete, my skating repertoire essentially consisted of going along, not falling over, turning gradually and doing an uncontrolled spinning stop. I was ready.

Prepped with rug-cutting skills and loaded with more shapes than even I could possibly throw, I was ready to find a roller disco. I had been in touch with the Dorset Sk8 Jam, which was happy for me to come along to their next session to showcase my new roller skating juggling show; better still, they were keen on me promoting it as part of The ABC Tour as *R is for Roller Disco*.

I had about a month to practice. During this time, I was also trying to get dates set for later in the tour. One of these dates was *T is for Trampoline*. I went to a trampoline park with Anton and his wife Angie to see if it would be possible for me to do a show there (and also, whilst we were there, have a bit of a play). As well as there being many trampolines, there was also a multitude of soft play equipment. We visited midweek, during the middle of the day, so we pretty much had the place to ourselves. One part of the soft play area was a three-lane obstacle course. You'd line up your friends (in my case, Anton and Angie), and then all shoot off down your individual lanes of the obstacle course, over foam triangles, squeezing through the large squidgy pasta-making rollers, across a zip line, then down a slide. There were cameras to track your times and the quickest time won.

I am very competitive and I gave it my everything. I was ducking and leaping and sliding and climbing at what felt like a world record pace. I think I may have even been going at an illegal speed. I was already thinking about my tweet that I was going to send to the famous physicist Brian Cox, telling him that I had shattered the speed of light, and then

CRACK!

I hear my ankle give way like a thick branch of a tree snapping. I landed like a sack of spuds on the floor.

But my time! I thought. I had been sure I was going to set a new world record that day. But alas, it wasn't to be. I dragged my sorry self through

the rest of the obstacle course, ankle aching like hell. I'll be honest with you, I have never been down a slide with such little oomph.

After tending to the ankle with ice, I felt I could walk on it again a little bit and, because I am incredibly stupid, I went trampolining. My ankle hurt but it wasn't unmanageable – at least until later that evening. I lay in bed with my ankle the size of a tennis ball and barely slept a wink.

The next morning, I hauled myself laboriously into an Uber and went to the hospital to get it looked at. It turns out that I had a very badly sprained ankle. As a result, we had to postpone *R is for Roller Disco* because, as a 29-year-old man, I was too determined to break speed records on a soft play obstacle course at a trampoline park.

After being on crutches, resting and regularly visiting my physiotherapist for a couple of months, *R is for Roller Disco* was finally rescheduled and I was ready to start training again. I was surprised at how quickly my roller skating skills came back considering, as I mentioned before, I wasn't a natural. Then again, I imagine my skill set would've come back quickly in pretty much anything if it had been as low as my roller skating ability.

The day of the show rolled around and Anton, Dan and I arrived at the venue. We arrived an hour early so that we could get ourselves used to the space and overcome any logistical hurdles that may be in our path.

Initially, we thought that we had arrived at the wrong place as we walked into what felt like an empty school hall. This was most likely due to the fact that it was an empty school hall. The disco wasn't yet set up so we decided not to panic too much.

However, by the time the roller disco began, nothing had changed. There were no disco lights. There was no DJ. There were no couples flirtatiously gliding around, holding hands and groping each other so they wouldn't fall over. A playlist from someone's iPad was playing through a small speaker and that was it. It remained a school hall, except it was quickly filling up with people that didn't want to boogie, slice rug or get down. These people were here to skate, and boy did they want to skate.

I had the sinking feeling that I had made a massive mistake. I was in a room with people that really wanted to just skate. They didn't particularly seem keen on having some juggler interrupting the one evening of roller skating practice they get in

a month. If anything, I felt like an inconvenience to them at best. I can imagine what the reaction of the jugglers at my local juggling club would be if someone came along to do a roller skating show, and we were forced to stop juggling to watch them.

I have never been to a roller disco, so I have nothing to compare it to. Maybe I expected too much. There were no disco balls, or coloured lights in sight, I didn't once hear anything from Earth, Wind and Fire's repertoire, and hardly anyone was falling over. This place was all roller, no disco. I messed up, but a lesson was learned: to assume makes a fool out of you and I.

Realising that we had to make the best of a tough situation, I decided that I would perform my juggling and roller skating as planned anyway, even if nobody watched. For filming, I suggested to Dan that he shouldn't go on skates as I didn't want him falling over and damaging the camera. He looked at me as if I had just told a seven-year-old him that Christmas Day was going to be cancelled this year and, instead, he'd be going back to school two weeks early.

After seeing how deflated he was, I caved, and let him skate. You should've seen his little face light up.

After skating around for a tense couple of hours, doing my juggling routines and trying to avoid being too much of a nuisance to the avid skaters, we took a short rest. Anton and I stood chatting to one of the organisers of the roller night as we watched Dan serenely gliding towards us, holding his £1,800 camera.

As he arrived to stop and chat, his skates had a different plan entirely. His feet slid from beneath him, and he fell flat to the ground, clutching onto his camera for dear life. As this happened the organiser, who was wearing hard plastic wrist guards, instinctively reached for Dan with one hand in an effort to catch him. To balance herself, her other hand flew through the air – wrist guard first – straight into my face clonking me good and proper on the snout.

My eyes began to stream; I was convinced I had a broken nose. I looked at Dan and he looked at me as if he knew what I was going to say.

"Was the camera rolling for that?" I asked. He looked ashamed and shook his head. As mentioned before, it was a challenging evening. The other difficulties of performing at a roller disco were sadly all of my own making. No, the roller disco wasn't a disco and no, they didn't really want me there. I should've paid the venue a visit long before I did the show, as I would've then realised these problems and found an alternative. If I ever do it again (which I won't), then it'd probably be best if I run my own night, which will be more disco than roller.

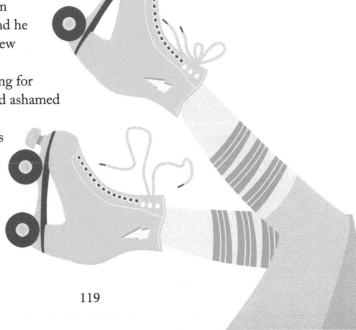

S IS FOR SNOW

S traight after setting a date for *R is for Roller Disco*, I began to think about booking a venue for 'S'. Ideally, I wanted to get to the point where the upcoming gigs were booked as far in advance as possible, but as with many things on The ABC Tour, it didn't work out that way. It turns out that booking gigs in places that don't normally host gigs is pretty tough. In all honesty, I wasn't too pleased with how *R is for Roller Disco* had gone, so I felt the need to redeem myself with the shows that followed.

Around this point, it struck me that the show didn't strictly have to be "good" for it to be entertaining. When I told stories from the tour, nobody wanted to hear "I performed in a Pig Pen and it went great!". They wanted to hear about how I got bit in the ass by a pig. Or how I was ignored by everyone at a roller disco. Or how Dan and I, for a cripplingly awkward moment, were the only people stark naked at a Naturist Resort.

It turns out that successes really aren't that funny. Belatedly, I came to the realisation that this tour was about the long game. Rather than just finishing the tour, my measure of success would come from having overcome the often self-inflicted difficulties I faced along the way.

With that in mind, I knew I needed to put myself in situations where I would be more likely to fail. I started to go through the suggestions:

STADIUM

People perform in
stadiums all the time.
Not challenging enough.

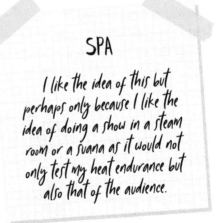

SPA

I like the idea of this but
perhaps only because I like the
idea of doing a show in a steam
room or a suana as it would not
only test my heat endurance but
also that of the audience.

SWIMMING POOL

I was so close to choosing this despite it being a logistical nightmare.

SEWER

Crap idea.

SKATE PARK

I love the unusual architecture of skate parks with all thier curves, twists and turns. If I had a day in a skate park I would like to try and come up with some

interesting ideas with rolling and bouncing balls. I've got nothing against this idea but others were better.

STRIP CLUB

I really like this idea but perhaps not for the reasons that you'd expect. I love the image of all the dancing platforms being taken up by the strippers apart from one,

upon which I'd do my show. It'd be interesting to see how the audience would react; I wonder if I'd be able to peel their eyes away from the scantily clad dancers to watch some juggling.

SNOW

Bingo.

I gravitated towards performing in the snow for a few reasons. The idea of challenging myself and seeing what my body was physically capable of doing in such conditions really appealed to me. I think it is visually interesting too, because it is rare that one gets to perform against such a blinding white background. Also, I love snow. Snow is exciting. Something about snow always reduces me to a childlike, giddy state.

The issue with wanting to perform in the snow was that it was May in the UK, and the chances of snow were pretty much zero. Even when it does snow in the UK, you can never really rely on top-quality flurries. Sometimes you may get an icy sludge, or perhaps an inch of snow that will bring the entire country to a halt. The ABC Tour budget was smaller than the possibility of snow in the UK in May, so travelling anywhere abroad was out of the question.

While recovering from my self-induced ankle sprain from the trampoline park, I set about trying to figure out if there was anywhere I could perform in a snowy environment. After a short burst of research, I managed to find a place called Snozone in Milton Keynes, which boasted that it was the UK's largest indoor real snow resort. Perfect!

As ever, I called them and gave them the usual ABC Tour spiel with as much charm as I could muster, and they seemed quite interested. I emphasised that I really would love to do the show soon as I was trying to do the entire alphabet in order, and I already had *R is for Roller Disco* set in the diary. A few days later I received an email saying that they'd love to go ahead and confirm a date. Excited like an otter at a waterpark, I replied straight away with a few date options, and eagerly awaited their response.

A week passed and it never came, so I followed it up with a phone call. They claimed to have not heard anything about The ABC Tour but they confirmed their interest and said they would email me. They didn't.

This pattern went on and on and on and on. I called. I emailed. I chased up emails. I chased up calls. I first got in touch with Snozone in May. I was in contact with them at least once a week for the next six months, after which I finally had a date for *S is for Snow* confirmed. Six months of effort just to book one show.

It is thanks to episodes like this that The ABC Tour took two years to complete. This is also the reason why 'S' ended up falling between 'U' and 'V', instead of its usual alphabetical habitat between 'R' and 'T'. I simply couldn't hold off the rest of the tour for so long.

Once the email-and-phone-call tennis match had come to completion, we finally reached the day of the show. Dan, Anton and I commenced the three-hour drive to Snozone. Anton had been googling what the temperature would be inside the zone, and he found out it was going to be −5°C. Yikes. That's certainly enough to feel it nipping at your nose. *But how bad could it be?* I thought.

As we walked into the building we could see the huge indoor ski slopes arching upwards before us. It really was quite magnificent. I was excited to figure out exactly how I was going to do a show in such a space. I did, however, notice a complete lack of posters about *S is for Snow*. Not only this but there were also no signs that there was a show of any kind happening today at all.

During the six month shemozzle to book this gig, I had sent posters and tagged Snozone in many social media posts, hoping that they'd spread the word. I guess I wasn't clear enough. If only we had tried to organise it for seven months, then perhaps there would've been some signs that a show was about to happen. I wouldn't hold my breath though.

Taking a moment to calm myself down, I sought out the manager so that we could figure out just how this show was going to work.

I introduced myself and said that I was here from The ABC Tour to do a show in the snow; she replied with "Sorry? What is it you'd like to do? Perform in the snow? I'm not sure this is going to be possible. Let me go and speak to someone about it".

The blood rushed to my face. I had been emailing for six months! Then we arrived after a three hour drive and there is no sign of a show happening. To add insult to injury, not even the manager knew that a show was supposed to happen. I honestly don't know how the message didn't get across. Perhaps they had new staff come and leave each week and the information for *S is for Snow* just happened to slip through the list of things to think about – every day – for half a year.

I had to do everything I could to not snap at the woman: I'm sure it wasn't her fault, she just hadn't been told. I cannot for the life of me understand how she, and everyone else, seemed to be left out of the loop. If I worked every day at an indoor snow centre and someone mentioned to me that something unusual was going to happen, like a juggling show in the snow, then I'm pretty sure I would remember it, but then again, I am biased.

We were led into a small room by the manager, and then left there twiddling our thumbs while she disappeared to try and find out some more information. The closer it drew to show time, the more frustrated I became. It was now twenty minutes until the show was scheduled to start and I still didn't know where or how the show was going to happen, or if it would even happen at all.

Pacing back and forth in the tiny room waiting for an update, I announced to Dan and Anton that if we didn't hear anything within the next five minutes, then we'd leave. I was angry, confused, raging and, honestly, quite sad. While waiting, I had decided that if we couldn't perform *S is for Snow*, then we'd just arrange a random time to go to the sea, film a few clips of me splashing about and trying to do a show and lazily call it *S is for Sea*. I really didn't want to do this as it felt like a cop-out. A few more minutes passed. I started putting my jacket back on with the intention of splitting.

Then the door opened. The manager entered with the news that we could go into the Snozone but we'd have to remain against the edge so we didn't get in the way of the skiers and snowboarders. Also, she informed us it was −10°C in there. Flipping heck! −10°C?!

"How cold can it be?" I asked breezily, only half kidding myself.

I really didn't like the idea of putting on a thick coat and snow trousers to perform in because then I'd blend in with everyone else. I decided to wear my three-piece suit – with long johns underneath – and a beanie hat. I don't know if you know this, but three-piece suits aren't known for their insulating capabilities. I was aware of this but, right then in that moment, that knowledge had momentarily escaped me.

Despite being driven by an angry stubbornness that I didn't really want to change my costume, I did think about changing my props. Usually, I juggle all-white props, because I think this looks nice and clean, it's versatile and visible against most backgrounds and there is no personality attached to it. If I had red sparkly rings, pink clubs or blue balls, then certain comments may be made. Little did I know that in −10°C, I'd be having at least one of those anyway (albeit mercifully hidden from view).

My point is that no one has anything to say about white props. They are neutral, like Switzerland or a High Court Judge. In the snow, however, I couldn't use white props as they'd blend into the background. As a result, and completely against Udry juggling fashion standards, I had to colour up the contents of my case.

Standing outside the snow zone, equipment in hand, we devised a plan as to how we could get in, set up, do the show, and leave in as tight an operation as possible. For obvious reasons, we didn't want to be in −10°C for one second longer than we needed to be.

You know that feeling when you go to take something out of the oven and heat from the oven smacks you in the face? This is what entering the Snozone was like, except intensely cold rather than baking hot. It wasn't like opening a fridge or a freezer, it was much, much worse. The cold didn't just hit you in the face, it engulfed you. It was even hard to breathe. So much so that my lungs felt like they were struggling to function. Unsurprisingly, my suit wasn't proving remotely effective against the conditions – but I did look cool!

The equipment was set up at world-record speed and I started the show immediately – no time for grandstanding here. To my surprise, there were a few people watching from the warmth of the cafe on the other side of the glass. Normally this was a viewing area to watch the skiers and snowboarders but, that day, for a small number of people, it was the viewing area from which to watch a tempered juggler freeze his bits off in an intemperate temperature.

I thought it'd be fun to start the show by doing my stripping-and-juggling routine, otherwise known as "str-uggling". It seemed ironic to open the show by removing an item of clothing in such an unforgiving climate. My logic was that even though I was removing an item of clothing, it is also a very physical routine, so I was gambling on the fact that my erratic movements

Photos: Anton Mackman

would compensate for the lack of a layer and, as such, I wouldn't feel much of a difference. I felt the difference. I have to be honest with you, I knew it'd be cold, but I didn't realise it would be that cold. I tend to cope quite well in frigid conditions. I actually like it. I'd prefer to be too cold than too hot. If you are chilly, you can always get warm by wrapping up or doing exercise. But if you are too hot, I personally find it really hard to cool down. However, even the constant full-body movement of me trying to take my jacket off whilst juggling didn't keep me warm in the slightest.

Amongst jugglers, rings are known for being the most painful on the hands of the three fundamental props (balls, rings and clubs). As my hands were starting to get a little numb, I decided I'd get my ring juggling routine out of the way next. As you might have guessed, the pain of the rings hitting my hands was incredibly intense. They felt like blades of several sharp bread knives cutting into my purlicues (the web of skin between your index finger and thumb).

   After a minute or so, a strange sensation occurred. My hands became so numb that the pain went away altogether and was instead replaced with a sort of "out-of-hand" experience. It felt like someone else's hands were

doing the juggling for me, such was the feeling of disconnect. Instead of me doing the work, it was a chubby fingered mal-coordinated chimp. My fingers moved slowly, I couldn't grip properly and I felt no sensation whatsoever. It was time to move on. Following my ring routine, I busted out a few necessary jumping jacks (not usually part of the act) and then I was on to clubs, where a very similar scenario took place and my hands were now actually starting to hurt with a long, dull ache.

I had to draw the show to an end. I was frozen to my core but thought: in for a penny, in for a pound. I finished the show by putting my jacket back on whilst juggling three balls. As I started, I forgot that quite a large section of this routine involves me laying down on the ground and juggling, occasionally rolling back and forwards like an upside down tortoise trying to get back on its feet. As soon as my behind came in contact with the snow, I knew this was a big mistake. Nevertheless, I'd done it now, so I might as well push on. As I rolled backwards and forwards whilst juggling balls through my legs, I felt the snow slip down my trousers and into my pants. I leapt up and briskly scrambled into my jacket. I was literally freezing my ass off.

Rapidly, we exited the snowy hellscape and returned to warm normality. As we walked, I felt the snow melting in my pants and dribbling down my leg. At least I hope that's what that was. Still fuming from the lack of organisation at the Snozone, we didn't hang around for niceties and got straight in the car to head home.

It had been such an unusual day. My emotions had been constantly up and down. The stress of trying to put this show on over six long months and then, when we'd finally arrived, realising that no one even knew why we were there, really got to me.

To make matters worse, after *Q is for Quiz* and *R is for Roller Disco*, this was the third excruciating experience in a row on The ABC Tour. There were still seven shows left and I wasn't sure how much more I could take. Quite appropriately, *S is for Snow* was at the bottom of a slippery slope of bad experiences. Surely, it couldn't get any worse, right? In the words of eighties pop star Yazz, "The Only Way is Up...Baby".

I really hoped she was right.

T IS FOR TRAMPOLINE

The three previous gigs on the tour were particularly challenging for their own set of reasons; *Q is for Quiz* was too long and I knew I could've done it better, I felt very unwelcome at *R is for Roller Disco* and *S is for Snow* didn't even know I existed. Once again I was feeling pretty disheartened about the whole project and I really needed a pick-me-up. I hoped that 'T' would bring some life back into the tour, so I carefully started sifting through the suggestions from my followers on social media:

TRAFFIC LIGHTS

Shows at traffic lights happen a lot in Europe and South America. The global popularity of this type of show meant that it didn't work for me on this tour.

TRAIN

The idea of doing mini shows for people up and down the carriages really appealed to me, but I didn't have that 'special something' I needed to keep me motivated about the tour.

TANK

Aside from getting hold of a tank, there were two issues. Inside a tank it doesn't look like one, while on top of a tank is no different from on top of a wall, or on top of a taxi – it adds little to the spectacle..

TELEPHONE BOX

I loved the thought of being in a telephone box with props. The show could be live-streamed onto the internet and people could call and request that I try various tricks while inside the box. Fun – but too similar to 'I is for Internet'

THEATRE

Oh, please! This suggestion is not welcome here.

TOY SHOP

I get a lot of inspiration for new routines from toy shops. I could forgive this being strictly 'S is for Shop' as the idea of a routine using only toys from the shop would be great.

TEA SHOP

Some of the reasons apply as with Toy Shop, except with the added bonus that I already have a routine with a teacup and tea bag. This would be a great opportunity to expand on that.

As enjoyable as it would be to perform in a Tea or Toy Shop, they would both be fairly safe bets and not particularly challenging at this point in the tour. To pull myself out of The ABC Tour funk that I had clumsily steered myself into, I needed something to really spice things up. I wanted a genuine

challenge and to push myself out of my comfort zone. Something just on the edge of (or maybe slightly beyond) my capabilities: *T is for Trampoline*.

After badly spraining my ankle at a trampoline park a few months before, it is hardly surprising that they weren't keen on letting me perform there. They said something about it being too dangerous.

I see their point. If I couldn't even visit the trampoline park without spraining my ankle, then why on Earth would it be safe to attempt a juggling show there? Instead of giving up on the idea and keeping myself safe, I decided to try Bristol's other trampoline park, Freedog.

The first thing I noticed about Freedog was its very hip vibe. Instead of the soft play area of the previous place, there were parkour obstacles that people were climbing up, balancing on and tumbling off. It was a trampoline park with a skateboarders' edge. Even taking my rejection by the previous venue into account, Freedog was by far my bouncerie of choice.

Putting on my most charming smile, I asked if I could speak to the manager. Doug emerged from his office, greeted me with a firm handshake and asked how he could help. Shifting myself into autopilot (I'd had a lot of practice by now), I

rattled off the classic ABC Tour spiel. I was taken aback when Doug eagerly agreed. This was the first bit of good news I had received from The ABC Tour in a while and I had forgotten what it felt like. I stuttered my response through a surprised grin and, when Doug offered to set a date there and then, I got that fantastic feeling that I'd met someone that believed in The ABC Tour as much as I did.

Doug was very enthusiastic about the whole idea, but then asked me about my previous trampolining experience. My palms started to sweat, as I figured that my response could be make-or-break for the show

taking place. I didn't want to lie because it would have been evident at a later date when he saw me clumsily struggling to bounce on my feet and panic whenever I was airborne. However, I feared that telling the whole truth about my complete inability might cause Doug to tone down his *joie de vivre* towards the tour, and I didn't want that.

"I don't have any trampolining experience at all," I shyly murmured. "No problem." he replied. "Let me give you and your friends a month's free membership so that you can get practicing for the show". Doug had just trumped his own awesomeness.

With the date set for *T is for Trampoline*, I had just under four weeks to learn how to get my bounce on. Looking for a coach, Nat Whittingham was recommended to me; someone who, as well as being a solid trampoline coach, was also a circus artist. I felt like he'd be the perfect coach for me as we have a slight crossover in worlds and, quite innocently, I thought that would make things easier. How wrong was I?

Photos: Anton Mackman

The training began and I had one specific goal in mind: I wanted to do some kind of flip.

By the end of the first day of training, it was humbling to know that I couldn't even bounce properly. Worse, I couldn't bounce properly on what is famous for being one of the bounciest of surfaces.

I was worse than I had expected. Nat, being the great coach that he is, was undeterred. He was great at breaking things down to its fundamental minutiae, not only preventing me from breaking my neck, but also from re-busting the fragile ankle I'd injured earlier in the year. After over an hour of bouncing, not only could I not do some kind of flip, but I also couldn't breathe.

It turns out that bouncing is hard work, especially when you are not as fit as Nat. The next two days were a complete write-off as I had a hard case of the full-body aches.

As the training wore on, I progressed to a level that I was proud of. Needless to say, this was not a very high level. My newfound abilities involved a few tricks (including a front somersault) but the best trick of all was that I could trampoline without gravely injuring myself. How I achieved the latter still puzzles me.

During this month, I also spent a lot of time figuring

out which routines I could perform on the trampoline, as well as learning how to do them. Luckily, a lot of my routines involve moving around and jumping about quite a lot anyway, so it wasn't too much of a stretch to try and adapt them to the trampoline – just 1,000 times more exhausting.

In my month of trampoline training, my body was never treated to an ache-free day. I started to forget what waking up pain-free felt like. Unlike Nat, my muscles didn't have muscles.

On the day of the show, Anton and I carted the equipment into the venue. We noticed the *T is for Trampoline* poster playing on the advertising TV. This poster had been popping up on the screen every time that we had

visited over the past month; Doug knew how to do things properly.

We set up the lights and sound in an appropriate corner of the trampoline park and decided to use four quadrants of trampolines as my stage space. This way I'd have the option of bouncing between trampolines, as well as standing on the criss-cross partition that separated them, as a backup plan if I couldn't do some parts of the show on the trampolines themselves.

About twenty people showed up to watch but, to be honest, that was a good turnout for this sort of thing. What was good about these twenty people was that they had chosen to come and watch the show. At the quiz, people wanted to do a quiz. At

the roller disco, people wanted to roll. In the snow, people wanted to ski. But here, as the trampoline park was closed, people had come specifically to see the show, which meant that, for the first time in a while, I was performing to a very supportive and enthusiastic bunch.

I delivered my intro into the microphone whilst bouncing up and down and, apart from a couple of minutes in the middle of the show, I didn't stop bouncing for the entire hour-long performance. Not only did I not stop bouncing, I was either talking or juggling at the same time throughout. By the time the show had finished, my energy canister was bone dry. Not a drop left. I was so exhausted that I was pretty sure I was going to throw up.

Even though this show sapped every drop of energy that I had, my routines more or less worked. I performed whilst bouncing on a trampoline, as well as using the trampoline skin to catapult my props. I bounced, I threw, I caught, I joked, I talked, they clapped, they cheered, they whooped, they laughed. Best of all, I landed two out of three flips. I consider this a success.

U IS FOR UNDERGROUND

Up until now, most of the venue choices had been specific places, such as a bakery, a castle or a forest. There were some exceptions, such as *S is for Snow* and *T is for Trampoline*, as these are things rather than places. That said, for the purpose of the tour, I think they still worked.

Yet there were a few linguistic loopholes that I was keen to avoid. When I received the suggestions for 'O', I instantly crossed out any "on top of" suggestions because I would be cheating the system. On top of a taxi is surely just *T is for Taxi*. Likewise, when I put the feelers out for suggestions for 'U', I had a similar issue with people putting forward options such as "Under a bridge" or "Under a table". It just felt like a cop-out. After all, I could just say under a roof and do it in a normal room. Discarding those suggestions, I sifted through the others:

UNIVERSITY

People regularly do shows at universities, so this option has no place on this tour

UP A TREE

I have the same issue with 'Up' as I do with 'Under'

UNDERTAKER'S

I'm trying to keep it light-hearted here

UNDERWEAR SHOP

A solid option but a bit too easy for this late in the tour. Also technically 'S is for Shop'

I was at my wit's end trying to come up with something, when two ideas came in that I particularly liked: "underwater" and "underground". It puzzled me as to why I felt these options were totally acceptable, but "under an awning" or "under a tree" were out of the question. Was it really the absence of the "a" that resolved the solution for me? Or perhaps the technical challenges that these posed? I think a little of both.

Once again, I was drawn towards the water. I desperately searched around for ways to make an underwater show work, but sadly, the solutions were too impractical. I'd love to have done a show fully submerged, with an audience joining me underwater, all of us in scuba gear.

I would learn to juggle heavy objects that would glide slowly through the water as the audience attempted a sluggish waterlogged applause. I could maybe try to find a way of communicating with them by using ultrasound like a dolphin. See? Impractical.

This left me with underground. I contacted a few tourist attractions with caves or mines, hoping that they would snap up the opportunity of a one-off random juggling experience. Sadly, they were either disinterested or concerned about health and safety. Both were valid reasons, but it was still frustrating.

A week later, my friend and fellow helper/booker/editor, Courtney, was doing a presentation about performance for camera and the uniqueness of the person vs persona for circus performers, as part of her MA for Directing Circus at Circomedia. In the presentation, she used video content from The ABC Tour to illustrate her points. It was the first time that I had seen the videos played in front of a live audience and it was comforting to know that viewers found it as funny as we did.

After the talk, I was approached by a man who had recognised me from the video screening, who congratulated me on the tour so far. He said he really loved the concept, then introduced himself as Gerry Cottle.

I was momentarily taken aback. This was GERRY COTTLE. The Gerry Cottle of circus fame. Gerry Cottle of Gerry Cottle's Circus, Cottle and Austen Circus, and the marvellous Circus of Horrors. Gerry revolutionised circus in the UK and, it is safe to say, was a BIG DEAL. At the time, Gerry ran a tourist attraction in Somerset called Wookey Hole, along with a small circus school with students performing live shows in the theatre, as Gerry Cottle's World Famous Wookey Hole Circus. However, the circus isn't the main attraction at Wookey Hole. It is most famous for its underground caves, billed as "the largest and most spectacular show caves in all of England". In a sweet little nutshell, the man who just approached me to tell me how much he likes The ABC Tour, owned a bunch of huge caves. This juggler-boy just landed on his feet.

I spoke to Gerry about me wanting to perform in his cave complex and he was thrilled with the idea. We exchanged contact details, arranged a site visit and, within the week, *U is for Underground* was set in stone.

I was joined on the day of the performance by several friends: in this instance, Dan, Anton and new to the team, Luke Bailey – a juggler/clown/performer that I met a few years ago and has since become a buddy. Luke was taking photos, Dan was filming and Anton was doing everything else that wasn't taking photos, filming or performing.

Having a team for this gig was essential because there was a ten-minute walk from the car park just to get to the entrance of the caves. Then getting into the caves involved navigating several steps, uneven surfaces and ducking through low-ceilinged passages. This would have been an utter nut-ache if I'd had to do it by myself, so I was very grateful to have my ABC Tour crew by my side.

We were guided deep into the guts of the caves by the delightful Wookey Hole staff, until we reached our cavernous performance location. After taking many small tunnels to get to this point, it was a relief when the space opened up to reveal one of the most beautiful caves in Wookey Hole's impressive collection. When we spoke, the echoes ricocheted off the cold, damp surfaces. To one side was a large, glistening lake with appropriately eerie underwater lighting that created shimmering effects against the ceiling. Occasionally you'd hear small drips of water plopping into the lake; its tiny ripples were emphasised in the silence.

Other than that, there was no noise. Not a peep. A Brian Eno atmospheric track would not be out of place here. The air was heavy and the thought of thousands of tonnes of earth sitting above this empty space made me feel a little uneasy. And of course, no phone signal. If there was an emergency, we were not getting out in a hurry.

Due to the minimal amount of ambient lighting, it was quite hard for us to see much at all. The lights were only just bright enough to inform you that you were actually in a cave. Undeterred, we jumped straight into the task of illuminating the space using small battery-powered industrial lights

with coloured gel filters. A quick sound and lighting test later, and I was ready for the show.

I was incredibly chuffed with how it all looked. The fact that we had actually been permitted to do a show in such a unique spot really blew my mind. The juxtaposition between the beauty of the cave, with the lights, the shimmering water and the shadows bouncing off the inconceivably ancient rock, in contrast with me, in a three-piece suit, about to do my twenty-first juggling and comedy show on a ludicrous tour, really made me happy.

Wookey Hole was open as usual for tourists to visit and partake in the cave tour. It was discussed that I would perform four ten-minute shows for visitors as they were ushered into my cave by their tour guide. Anton, Dan, Luke and I waited patiently for our audience to enter our newly lit showroom. Due to the deathly silence, we could hear them drawing nearer for more than ten minutes before they excitedly arrived.

I performed four new sections of material that I'd created with this particular show in mind. The first was a club routine using glow clubs with flashing LED lights in them[16]. The glow clubs looked marvellous and scattered a number of interesting shadow effects upon the cave's lumps and bumps.

---

[16] *Generally, I never perform glow clubs as a solo act. I will occasionally perform a glow club routine with Gandini Juggling, but this will be something that I haven't created, I haven't had to programme the clubs, and am not in charge of any of the equipment. These are all tasks that I just don't want to do. Besides the logistical pain that they cause, I am not a fan of glow clubs or any type of LED entertainment, for that matter. I like very few acts that use lights in their props in order to attempt to enhance the viewers' experience. You could have someone standing there just doing a basic three club juggle, but because they are using glow clubs, the clubs are changing colour in time with the music, flashing, strobing and making pretty trailing light patterns in the air, the audience loves it. They will love it more than someone doing crazy cool tricks with three "normal" clubs, despite the latter being much harder to do.*

In my opinion, LED juggling can often be used as a mask for lack of skill, and it's for this reason that I am not a fan. That being said, if a computer programmer got in touch and wanted to collaborate in making a routine together where I would be in charge of the juggling and he would be in charge of programming the clubs to make them look cool, I could be convinced by the idea. However, I think computer programmers probably have better things to do with their time than to mess around with juggling.

Photos: Luke Bailey

Next was a semi-improvised ring juggling routine using my iPad.
I have a fantastic app called BeatWave, which I used to create music
whilst juggling. It consists of a 16x16 grid of squares with each square
making a note or beat. A time-bar consistently passes over the grid
from left to right on repeat. When one of the squares is touched, it
becomes highlighted and parps out its note every time the time-bar
passes over it. The music created is very minimalist and atmospheric.
The echoes of the cave really helped bring its eeriness alive. Whilst
juggling or balancing the rings, I tapped the screen of the iPad to
add another note to the track so that the music builds as the routine
progresses.

After the ring routine, I awkwardly spent a minute or so preparing
myself for my next section. My third piece involved three head
torches; one attached to each leg, pointing upwards, and one on my
head worn in the conventional manner. This created an unusual effect
as the uplighting from my knees made me look haunting, in the same
way that a torch under your chin would during spooky stories around
a campfire.

I then proceeded to perform a three-ball juggling routine using
white balls, trying to make them pass through my new beams of lights
by throwing around my leg and over my head. I still think this is a
good idea, but for this show, I was lit too brightly for it to have the
effect I'd wanted. Instead, I just looked like a nonconformist miner on
his lunch break.

I mentioned in the previous chapter that I love spending time in
toy shops and that I find a lot of inspiration for routines in them. A
couple of months prior, I was in a toy shop in Bath when I saw a guy
control a flying toy with only his hand. Nothing in his hand, not even
a control. The toy was made up of a clear plastic ball, about the size of
a golf ball, with flashing lights inside (for the kids), and topped with
two mini helicopter propellers. I wasn't surprised when I found out
that this mysterious beast was called a Heliball. It's a lot catchier than
the other option, Ballcopter.

Keen to learn more, I quizzed the Heliball pilot about his craft.
He kindly explained that it was controlled by a light sensor on
the base of the ball. When the ball senses it is close
to your hand, it will fly itself back up a few metres,
before descending once more. The toy pilot hit me
with his salesman niceties, and within a matter of
minutes, I had bought three of them. I spent the

next few weeks working towards getting my Heliball licence so that I could figure out how to do a juggling routine with my new, tax-deductible toys.

U is for Underground provided a perfect opportunity to premiere my new Heliball finale. The batteries were charged and I started the engine. The propellers whirred, thrusting the flashing ball up towards the cave top, before then descending down to its fleshy landing pad, at the perfect timing in the gap of my ball juggling pattern. In rehearsals, Heliball would start to soar upwards before it touched my palm, giving it that magical levitating effect that I fell in love with at the toy shop.

Perhaps it was stage fright but, on this occasion, Heliball didn't levitate and instead came crashing down towards my hand where I was forced to slap it back upwards for another go. It came down once more and hit my palm again. *Bad Heliball.* The second hand-slap caused the mischievous flying fool to fly out of control, sending it bouncing along the rocky ground of the cave towards the audience.

Startled, as you would be, an audience member batted the badly behaved buzzing boy away from the crowd, back towards me. Though I was just an amateur pilot at this stage, I tried everything I could to regain control of the vessel, but it seemed to have a mind of its own. It was as if the flying toy couldn't even see my hand in this dark and dingy cave. It turns out that it couldn't, because WE WERE IN A DARK AND DINGY CAVE!

Still buzzing around and causing chaos like a wasp at a birthday party, Heliball flew away from the audience and myself and plopped straight into the lake, where it twitched and glowed for a few moments before it went to sleep. *Very bad Heliball.*

With my tail between my legs, I fished the troublesome toy out of the lake before packing up the rest of my props, shutting down the lights, and heading out of the cave the same way we came in. Climbing the steps towards the light of the outside world, we crossed paths with another group on a tour. The tour guide had miscounted how many shows we agreed that I'd do, and had told his group about the juggling show they were going to witness in a cave.

They seemed quite gutted that I was all packed up, so I decided to unpack a few props and do a mini show for them on the steps. The steps were uneven (isn't that the very nature of steps?), and had a shallow stream unexpectedly flowing over it. Even with my previous ABC Tour experience, this was a less than ideal place to be doing a show. I performed, they clapped, and then it was finale time.

As my usual cave finale was now soaked through, I performed a trick where I juggled six rings (on the wet uneven steps!) and caught them all around my neck. I then got a kid to stand behind me with his hand in the air and then I flicked all of the rings off of my head, and they landed on his arm.

That's what was supposed to happen. Instead, I gave it a little too much oomph, the rings overshot the kid's arm and he took the pounding of all six rings straight to his face. I turned around to see him smiling, with all of his teeth. Phew!

The lessons I learned from this day was to not use light-sensitive toys in the dark, and when it comes to performing in a stream on the steps, maybe audience participation isn't the best option.

After bouncing back from the foul trilogy of 'Q', 'R' and 'S' with the success of both *T is for Trampoline* and now *U is for Underground*, I really felt like I had my ABC Tour groove back. With only five more shows left, I approached the next show – 'V' – with a skip in my step, feeling that the tour was finally back on track.

V IS FOR VAN

Various options were available for 'V', such as vineyard, velodrome or vault, but nothing resonated with me more than a van. I had learned from some of the less successful shows on the tour, that whenever the venues weren't too engaged with the idea, there were few opportunities to improve the performance. At *K is for Knitting Club*, *T is for Trampoline*, and *N is for Naturist Resort* – to name but a few – the owners had trusted me with the show and given me full control over the venue. As a result, these shows turned out great. Where there was resistance and I had no control, such as *R is for Roller Disco* and *S is for Snow*, the shows were not as good.

By doing a show in a van, I would have full control. I could transport the venue to a variety of different people in a short space of time and this really appealed to me. I also loved the challenge of performing to small numbers of people in very close proximity. I developed my liking for this type of show during *J is for Jail* and was keen to try something similar again.

With the idea lodged deep into my brain, it was time to pursue it. I went down to the van-hiring place (which will remain

142

nameless for reasons that will become apparent later) to enquire about hiring a van just for a day. I felt like I had to bend the truth a little bit, as I didn't think they would be keen on hiring out a van to somebody who was going to be doing performances in it, and rightfully so. I rolled off a bunkum story about how I was moving house and that I had a lot of heavy furniture, so I'd needed a van with a tail lift. In reality, the tail lift was to help get people into the van, if we so needed it. I perused the options and selected the "vanue." I reserved it and I was on my merry way.

To be abundantly clear: I reserved the van. I made the reservation. The van was reserved for me, for a certain date. I had reserved the van.

With a date and a van now booked, I started promoting the show on social media, asking people to suggest locations I could drive to and perform. I was inundated with suggestions and I knew straight away that I wouldn't be able to do all of them, so I decided to choose the most contrasting options that'd make for the most interesting story.

I live on a quiet little cul-de-sac in Bristol that contains fifteen houses. I mean no disrespect to the people who live here, but I am the youngest on my street by approximately 35 years and I love it. I have the type of old-school neighbours that you see in films: the type that wave to you across the street and will – without fail – send you a Christmas card. They always say hello when I see them and their curtains always twitch when I leave or return to my house.

Apart from the annual Christmas cards that I send out, I don't feel like I do enough for my lovely neighbours; therefore, I thought that *V is for Van* could be a good opportunity to show them a little bit of what I do and to try and bring the residents together for a small event. I hand-wrote fourteen letters telling them about the show and posted them to each house on my cul-de-sac. It went a little something like this:

> Hello. My name is Jon and I am a juggler and a comedian. I live at number 2. Next week on the 14th November, I am going to be doing a show in a van out on our street at 10am, and you are officially invited. I know it sounds weird, but come along. Trust me, it'll be fun. I'll supply biscuits. See you there. From your trusty neighbour at number 2,
>
> Jon.

By the time *V is for Van* rolled around, I was well prepared for what I hoped would be a long but thrilling day ahead. With the possibility of the cul-de-sac clan soon to arrive, it was time to pick up the van. Anton, Dan and I arrived at the van-hiring place to pick up our van and, hell-on-a-bike, there was no van.

Unless things weren't clear, I had made a reservation. A van had been reserved. However, the van I had reserved just wasn't there. They had somehow hired it to someone else, rather nullifying the whole reservation concept. The show was happening in 90 minutes, and we didn't even have a venue. They told us they could offer another van without the tailgate but, like I had stressed earlier, I had some very awkward furniture – and octogenarians – that I needed to hoick into the van. Without a tailgate, it'd be very tricky, hence the reservation I'd made.

We decided that, in order to save a little bit of time, Dan and I would go back to my house and get everything ready, so that when Anton sorted the van, he could drive it to us and we'd be ready to rock and roll straightaway. At 9:55 am I called Anton again, but there was still no news. The show was due to start in five minutes, and the van depot was at least fifteen minutes drive away.

We were on the brink between cancelling and postponing. I ran into some of my neighbours on the street who had come to watch, and I had to tell them that it was going to be pushed back a bit later and to keep their peeping eyes peeled through the curtains, as per usual, for a van arriving at any moment. My phone buzzed and it was exciting news: Anton had secured a van and was on his way.

I was in costume, with my props and equipment next to me, as Dan and I waited on the pavement for our vanue to arrive. As I saw Anton pull around the corner in a van that was absent a tailgate, I knew that the day was going to be full of the good kind of chaos. He parked up the white beast, we gave the inside a quick brushing down and then we hauled the equipment inside to try and rapidly create a vanue for our eager crowd. Ten minutes later, and it was showtime.

For the first show of the day, eight members of the cul-de-sac crew approached the van, where I beckoned them in. Some of them seemed shocked, and perhaps frightened, of the idea of getting in the van. Especially Dot, who was 82 and had recently had a hip operation. Fear not, as Anton and I lugged her in like a delicate piece of luggage.

The show went down a treat and, despite the complications of performing inside such a small space, it wasn't too challenging from a technical perspective. The ceiling was low enough that if I did a small jump, I'd hit my head and if I

were to do a twirl in a flamenco dress, the dress would hit the sides of the van and the legs of the people watching. With this knowledge in mind, it would have to be a non-jumping and non-twirling-in-a-flamenco-dress kind of show.

Personally, I liked the challenge that the restrictions created. Fifteen successful minutes later, we unpacked the audience from the van, each a little happier but relieved to be free. I had given those eight people something else to talk about during the day – and perhaps the week – and I'd even given them biscuits to nibble on during the show. So, in that sense, I consider the first stop to have been a blinding success.

For our next stop, we were hitting the opposite end of life's bell curve and heading to a nursery to attempt to perform *V is for Van* to a bunch of toddlers. This is as unusual as it sounds. My friends and circus couple Loz James and Marky Jay (who lent me the quiz for *Q is for Quiz*, and the fire clubs for *C is for Castle* and *F is for Forest*) had hooked me up with the chance to perform at Times for Tots Nursery, which is where they regularly took their child during the day. Loz informed the parents of the children at the nursery in advance about the arrival of a van and that there was going to be a free comedy and juggling show inside. The Bristolian parents, being the bohemian, free-spirited, delightful lot that they are, were all totally on board with the idea.

The issue here wasn't that I was getting a bunch of toddlers into a van for a show, the problem was that I cannot perform for kids. I have never been able

to handle children as a crowd. They are not particularly into my material and I am stubborn enough that I am not prepared to adapt it for them.

In order to be able to deal with this cacophony of kids, I needed some tips. I sought advice from Marky, who is a fantastic children's entertainer. I highly recommend him for children's birthday parties if you are in the East Bristol area, whether you are a parent or not. His three golden rules for performing with kids are as follows:

1. Kids are the most honest present audience you will ever be in front of. If you're bombing, there is no reason other than that they fundamentally don't like you as a person. Take what you want from this information.

2. By default, you are an authority figure. Undermine that position and they will love it. Everything from falling over to not knowing an animal fact.

3. As a juggler, you are close to being magical. They literally don't have the motor skills you have, so never under-sell your tricks. However, if they have seen your trick already, but performed on a unicycle, they will be sure to tell you.

With Marky's advice loaded into my arsenal, I thought I was ready to take these toddlers on. Said toddlers and parents were quickly crammed into the van while the remaining audience peered in through the ajar backdoors. The show started and within less than a minute, a child started crying.

I rightfully took this as a personal attack, as I hadn't even started juggling yet. After one child started crying, another joined in to create whatever the opposite of a pleasant harmony is. Then, like popcorn kernels in a pan of sizzling oil, they all started going off.

Marky's rules weren't working for me and, annoyingly, I knew he was watching and would have been able to tame this wild beast with a click of his fingers. I was struggling to maintain control and to be heard over the clamour, so I did what I thought was best in the situation: I cranked up some music, performed a routine, and drowned out their downbeat din.

After fifteen of the longest minutes of my life, the show was over, and we herded the families out. From my experience at the monkey sanctuary, the pigpen and now this – I completely understood the famous W.C. Fields quote, "Never work with children or animals. They are scene stealing and completely unpredictable".

Exhausted from my short-lived fifteen-minute career entertaining kids, I left with even more respect for children's entertainers than I ever had before. I knew that good children's entertainers were highly skilled, but never realised the fortitude it takes to control a crowd of crying kids. It's a skill that I just don't have. Feeling drained, we had a little snack and then decided to head to Circomedia: the top school for contemporary circus and physical theatre training in the UK, where I occasionally teach. It was lunchtime for the students and I thought this would be the perfect time to try and get a load of them into the van.

On arrival, I entered the main training space and announced: "I am going to be doing a show in fifteen minutes in that van. Come along and bring as many people as you can". I sometimes rhyme when talking to groups of students.

During their two or three year course, the Circomedia students get put through a lot. As well as training incredibly hard, they also get pushed to the limit mentally, with modules such as clowning, burlesque and stand up comedy. These modules can be immensely tough and have been known to regularly bring people to tears. Emotionally, they can be very draining and I have nothing but respect for Circomedia for just how far they push the students and inspire the students to push themselves.

As a result, this creates a very resilient group of talented individuals that are always up for a challenge. With this knowledge in mind, I wanted to see how many of them I could get into the van for the next show. We packed them in tightly like sardines. The students used their initiative to create more space for others, by leaving their backpacks outside in a pile. We eventually managed to cram in twenty-six, making me the twenty-seventh person in the van.

I waited in the very limited performance space for Dan, the twenty-eighth person, to squeeze in, so that he could film the show from behind the student cluster. During the two previous shows of the day, I had left the van doors open. I felt like it would have been irresponsible and unpleasant to close the doors once the elderly or toddlers were inside; however, I felt like the sturdy students would be keen on the idea.

With all twenty-eight of us stuffed into the sweatbox together, we closed the doors. The inside of the van was smaller than the jail cells at *J is for Jail* but contained more than two times as many audience members. This was the most intimate show I'd done yet. Looking at the students from the lit-up stage end of the van, they were packed in so tightly that they were almost on top of each other. It was like looking at a page of a "Where's Wally?" book, but without the Wally.

As well as being smaller than the jail cell, it was also stuffier than a jail cell – and no airflow. Even though it was a minute amount, each breath was slightly more of a strain as we were all sharing the same limited supply. The condensation was building up on the ceiling and walls. The claustrophobic levels were starting to increase.

Fifteen minutes in, I could tell that the audience was starting to become uncomfortable. Fidgeting amongst each other. Saying things like, "I'm starting to become uncomfortable". As I have been performing for over twenty years, I have developed the ability to magically be able to pick up on such subtleties from an audience, so I quickly brought the show to a close. After twenty exciting and excruciating minutes with an irresponsible amount of people in a van, the show finished. When the back doors of the van opened, the gush of fresh air that greeted us was very welcome. We were freed.

Unintentionally, I had scheduled myself to perform for three generations of audiences on the same day. It was now early afternoon and as we had the van for the rest of the day, we thought it would be a shame to return it so early. We had ticked off the three shows in the schedule, so now, any others would be a bonus.

We drove to a large retail car park surrounded by a variety of different shops. My theory was that a variety of shops would attract a variety of people. We parked up and prepped the van. Now I just needed an audience. With an air of innocence, I approached a random family passing through the car park and attempted to give them my best "I'm doing a show in that van, do you want to come and see it?" pitch. I asked families, couples young and old, and friends on shopping days out, all of them, unsurprisingly, declining my offer.

Naive as I may be, I was aware of how the offer sounded, but it didn't stop me from trying. Stupidly, I thought that if I could just do a show for one group, then the news would spread and people would be lining up for as far as the eyes could see to get into the van. This was not the case. Everybody said no.

Even looking at the dodgy white van, with a painted ABC Tour sign stuck to its exterior with magnets and industrial lighting on the inside to give it that show biz razzle-dazzle feel, fun disco music blaring from a speaker, and the offer of "I'm doing a show, want to come and see it in the van?", I was convinced that it wasn't the concept that was the problem, it was the people. In retrospect, I can see that I had convinced myself that there was no problem with the idea at all. I foolishly generalised that the type of people at a retail park wouldn't be the type of people to see a show in a van. Whatever that means.

We packed up and drove our vanue to a car park of an organic health food store and a craft shop. I wanted to find the freewheeling, bohemian, up-for-anything types that I know and love, and that Bristol is famous for. These people were my type of people, and I know that they like to hang around craft shops, cafes and health food stores. I know this because I am one of them. And if someone came up to me and said, "Hey man, I'm doing a show in this van, do you want to come and see it?", I would be first in line.

We parked up and I started to offer the show to the first people that I saw, and I was greeted with the familiar rejection that I had been receiving all afternoon. I needed to change my tack. I said to the next couple: "Hello. I am doing an art project where I am doing a short and snappy juggling show in this van. Would you like to see one?". Much to my surprise, they immediately said yes.

It seemed that changing the word from "show" to "art project" made it more acceptable in the eyes of the approached. I wasn't exactly lying: The ABC Tour is an art project. It's a project, within the arts. Whatever it was about the rephrasing, it worked. Maybe it's because arty types like myself always want to try and support the arts, even if it is in a dodgy white van. Or maybe the word "show" can have quite negative connotations. If I say, "I'm doing a show in a van", maybe this could be misconstrued as, "I want to show you something in the van", which could easily be miscomprehended as perverse. I am not exactly sure: all I know is that the new phrasing worked from then on out. We even had a couple come and watch a show with their one-week-old baby.

Despite the rocky start, the day went tremendously well in the end. I had performed for the residents in my cul-de-sac and for the toddlers at a nursery. I irresponsibly crammed twenty-six students into a van for an uncomfortable amount of time, and I had even managed to convince a number of strangers to get in to watch the show. We didn't get the van we wanted but we made it work, way beyond our expectations.

Anton wasn't happy with returning the van without some kind of faux complaint about how it really messed up our day. Without the tailgate we couldn't move the made-up furniture to my new made-up house. Anton prides himself in being an exceptional blagger, and this time he did not disappoint. He managed to get us a full refund on the use of the van.

W IS FOR WINDOW

Weird shows were starting to feel like the norm for me by this point in the tour. Whenever I would perform one of my "regular" shows, the equipment that I once took for granted started to feel like a luxury. I found myself remarkably grateful for standard amenities, such as a lighting rig and professional technicians to operate them.

With my usual shows, sometimes I am so fortunate that I can request for any lighting set up that I want and there will be a qualified technician there to make it happen, instead of plugging in a set of industrial work lights that would always be too hot and too bright, meaning we'd have to find surfaces to reflect them off and make sure they were not leaning against anything flammable.

Theatre stages are normally quite large, with more space than I could possibly need in height, depth and width, which means I have the flexibility to perform whatever material that I want. In most of The ABC Tour gigs, there were limitations of one kind or another as to which material I could perform, what props I could use, and occasionally, how long I could even remain on the "stage" (as happened in *S is for Snow*).

With only four more shows to go, the end of the tour was in sight. By this point, it was getting tricky to choose venues that were notably different from the previous twenty-two. I was now onto 'W' and I needed some inspiration for ideas, so I called upon the reliable social media world for suggestions:

WOODS

Nice, but just too similar to F is for Forest.

WAKE

Apart from being hugely inappropriate, it would also be a logistical nightmare to organise. I wouldn't want the tour held up because someone didn't die as quickly as we had expected.

WIND TUNNEL

I love this suggestion. If I were to do a show in a wind tunnel, I'd need access in advance to see what is possible. I imagine that one could create some great effects using the wind as a tool, such as throwing props into the wind so they would return like boomerangs.

WRESTLING RING

Another solid suggestion. I love the idea of performing in the interval of a wrestling match, and then planning for a wrestler to come out and break a chair over my back. What a finale that would be!

From the suggestions, my first choice was a wrestling ring. After looking into the UK wrestling scene, unfortunately, it was the off-season, which meant that if I was going to perform at a wrestling match, then I'd have to delay the tour by at least another six months – and I really didn't want to do that.

My second choice was the wind tunnel, and I happened to know that there is one in Bristol. I got in touch, and it's fair to say they were far from keen on the idea.

I was back to square one. It was disheartening to be banging my head against a brick wall so close to the end of the tour. Whenever I get stuck in a rut, I normally whack my headphones on and aimlessly walk. I find that the combination of listening to music and consciously taking in my surroundings often helps dislodge any ruttiness.

It was early November in Bristol, which meant that the city was eagerly preparing itself for Christmas (I do love the festive season but does it really have to last for one sixth of the year?). Whilst silently bickering to myself about the insidious creep of Christmas into other parts of the year, I happened to walk past the elaborate window displays of Harvey Nichols and John Lewis. The penny dropped. Of course: *W is for Window.*

Anton's goddaughter, Nancy, happened to work at a high end department store called Harvey Nichols, so the next day we popped in with our finest schmoozing hats on. She asked the management about me doing a show in their window display, and of course, they said no. Artists work on the concepts and designs of these window displays for months on end. Why on earth would they let "Jonny Juggler Boy" go in and mess that up? I was aware that it was the longest of shots but it was worth a try.

After a few more failed attempts at getting myself into a window display, I accepted defeat. Understandably so – retailers are precious about their window displays. If I was going to be performing in a window, it would have to be an unoccupied one.

I walked around the city centre, making a note of all of the empty window displays that I could find, then went home and methodically contacted them. I was rejected by all but one; a window situated in The Galleries, a shopping centre smack bang in the heart of Bristol. It housed three floors with a plethora of shops, including one that – fortunately for me – was empty.

After receiving my email, the manager, Cameron, replied saying that they were keen on letting me use the empty shop for *W is for Window*, and that we could do the show whenever we wanted. Cameron is what I would describe as a **MEGA DUDE**. A yes man. He gets things done.

Keen to keep the tour moving along, we scheduled the show to take place in a week's time. My usual suspects for helping me out – Sam, Anton, Dan, Courtney, and Luke – were all busy and I really didn't fancy doing a show this late on in the tour by myself. After a shout out on Facebook for some assistance, one of my students from Circomedia got in touch, Will Huddy.

Will is a couple of years older than me and we always got on in class as he was a good student, hard working and had very creative ideas. Luckily he was available, as he was the perfect candidate to help me out for this show.

I have a six-foot-tall male mannequin called Manny. Don't ask why. I just do. I felt like Manny would really help zhoosh up the window display. As you know from *V is for Van*, I live in a particularly snoopy cul-de-sac. I would love to know what my neighbours were thinking as I stuffed Manny's disembodied limbs into the boot of my car. With no disrespect to Manny, he is quite the creepy figure. When I first bought him, I stood him up in

Photos: Will Huddy

the centre of my living room. I then went to make a cup of tea in the kitchen and, when I returned a few minutes later, I forgot he was there and he scared the actual faeces out of me. I have since used Manny on countless occasions to scare people. It's what he does best.

First thing in the morning, I headed off to pick up Will and made the short journey into Bristol's bustling city centre to the Galleries, with the car filled with props, equipment and mannequin limbs. After parking the car and filling ourselves up with coffee, we introduced ourselves to the shopping centre's manager and all-round **MEGA DUDE**, Cameron. **CAMERON MD** escorted us to the empty shop where I was going to perform *W is for Window*, and was incredibly accommodating. Firstly, he lent us a shopping trolley to lug our bits and bobs from the car park to the window. The shop was empty – a completely blank canvas – and he gave us free rein to do whatever we wanted with it. We explained to **CAM MD** that, ideally, we'd like some kind of backdrop to help spice up the window display. I also asked if, on the off chance, he had a mannequin stand, as I had annoyingly left an essential part of Manny's base at home. Within ten minutes, he returned with a selection of backdrops, a mannequin stand, and a zimmer frame (and I quote), "just in case you needed it". Who has a spare mannequin stand and brings a zimmer frame just in case you need it? **CAMERON THE MEGA DUDE** – that's who.

Sadly the mannequin stand was too big for Manny's leg hole; instead, we had to tape it to his leg like a coquettish garter. Dirty Manny. Setting up the display was an exciting experience as we could see first-hand the intrigue of the passers-by through the window as the display developed. I am saying window display in the loosest sense of the word.

When I think of window displays, I think of the extravagant works of art that you would find in Harrods, John Lewis or Selfridges. I don't need to tell you that this certainly wasn't at that kind of level. This was two guys with a bunch of random stuff and one hour, trying to turn

a blank space into something that people might want to glance at.

After an exhausting set-up, the backdrop was up, The ABC Tour sign prominently displayed, an erected and clothed mannequin put in place, helium balloons inflated and lights on. It was finally time to start the show.

The show started, or did it? It certainly didn't feel like the start of a show. Similar to the feeling I had before *I is for Internet*, there was no buzz from an excitable audience; in fact, there was no buzz at all. There was an audience, but a physical barrier separated us. The window was situated at the bottom of an escalator, which was very handy as people could watch the action as they were descending. However, this was bad in the sense that, if too many people stopped at the bottom of the escalator to watch, it created a cluster that would block the exit of said escalator. The security guard on duty made sure that if there were too many people, they would soon get moved along.

I wanted people to watch, but the moment there were too many people, they were told to leave. The security guard and myself had completely opposing goals in this scenario which, as you can imagine, made things quite tricky.

On top of this, my amplifier was on the outside of the window so that it'd grab the public's attention, but my

microphone and iPad – from which I controlled the
music – were on the inside of the window. When I spoke
into the mic, I could only hear my voice in the room and
to me, it sounded like the amp wasn't even on. Similarly,
when I played the tracks I could barely hear them. It was
as quiet as sitting near somebody on a bus, whose music
you can faintly hear through their headphones. I could
hear it only if I didn't move, breathe or blink.

When I addressed the audience, I could see them
listening and responding, but I could hear nothing of
their reaction. I was starting to empathise with how
the fish must have felt at *A is for Aquarium*. Whenever
I was juggling, my eyes were obviously preoccupied, so
the deathly silence made it feel like there was nobody
watching. Not only that, it felt like there was nobody
around at all, in the entire shopping centre, or even in the
city. The silence made the time drag, and the show was
unenjoyable to perform, to say the least.

In an odd way, I didn't mind that it was such a painful
experience because I'd known what I was getting myself
into. There was a soundproof barrier between the people
I wanted to entertain and myself; the silence inside the
shop wasn't that dissimilar from the quietude of the
empty jail cell at The Island in Bristol, where I performed
J is for Jail.

With the time moving so slowly, I kept checking in with Will to see how long I had performed for. His reply was always at least half of what I thought I had endured. With *I is for Internet* the audience were watching online, so I performed in a crowd-less room. That show was strange because I couldn't hear the public's response, but the tension was alleviated because I was in a room with four of my friends, so it wasn't too bad.

Yet with *W is for Window* I was all alone. Will was nearby, admittedly, but he was often filming from afar, so I only saw him a couple of times during the forty-minute performance. I could hear myself breathing. I'm sure I could hear my heart beating too, although there is a good chance that my memory exaggerates. That, or I needed to urgently seek medical attention.

When the show finally ended it was a huge relief. Even though it had been a mentally painful experience, people did watch. The audience was aware that I couldn't hear them so made an extra effort to communicate visually with thumbs up and the like. Taken as a whole, I can look back proudly at *W is for Window*. I had performed a show that was incredibly hard on me mentally, that had pushed me excruciatingly far out of my comfort zone. This was exactly what The ABC Tour was meant to be about. My discomfort only made it more of a triumph.

X IS FOR XMAS

X-Ray Clinic and xylophone were the only two words I could think of that began with 'X', after an embarrassingly long amount of time spent brainstorming. An X-Ray clinic could have worked logistically, but I felt it would be insensitive to attempt to do a show for people that were nursing injuries. Something tells me that they might not be in the mood for a comedy juggling spectacle.

I briefly entertained the idea of performing my show behind a large X-Ray screen so that the audience could just see my skeleton and my props, but then I remembered just how harmful it is to be exposed to X-Rays for prolonged periods of time – so that was out. I liked the idea, but I don't like it enough to harm myself for, let's face it, an inevitably small crowd.

As for 'xylophone', I guess I could've tried to get my hands on a large xylophone to perform a show on, but even in this context, it seemed a bit boring. After stumbling through a sloppy version of *Frère Jacques* by bouncing juggling props off its keys, I would then just be stood on an annoyingly noisy surface that would plink and plonk with every footstep throughout the rest of the show.

I also considered the possibility of performing in the xylophone department of a music shop, before I realised that I have been to quite a few music shops, and have never once noticed a dedicated xylophone department.

Courtney came up with the idea of doing *X is for X Marks the Spot*, where we could do a treasure hunt that would lead to a show. We'd secretly film the audience undertaking the treasure hunt with me popping up every now and then in disguise to give them clues. I loved this idea and Courtney had planned treasure hunts before, so it was perfect. Sadly, by the time it came to put this show together Courtney was back in the United States as her visa had run out. As Christmas is a busy time of year, finding the time to design a treasure hunt – let alone learning how to design one – was just too much work. Especially if Harvey was expecting his bi-annual Christmas card.

A part of me was also drawn to the idea of doing *X is for X-Rated Show*. I had an image of performing in my three-piece suit in a sexy dungeon of a BDSM club, before a group of leather-clad dominatrices who were politely applauding and cheering as they sat upon their gagged, submissive slaves. Any time the subs would show signs of enjoying the show, the doms would crack the whip and soon put a stop to their jollity.

I loved this idea but I also knew that the content would be considered too sensitive to be viewed for the online series, and I didn't want to have to give an age-appropriate warning to the episode.

As Hallowe'en had just finished, it was fast approaching Christmas time; by which I mean, it was early November. The halls were being decked, the German Christmas market was in full flow in Bristol's city centre, and a temporary ice rink was being installed. Everywhere you looked, there were signs of Christmas in its many forms: Merry Christmas, Feliz Navidad, Seasons Greetings, Holidays are comin', Joyeux Noël… it's Xmas time.

Wait, it's Xmas time?

Xmas! If Tesco's can get away with using Xmas instead of Christmas, then so can I. I have always been a sucker for Xmas Markets, so I contacted the best Xmas market that I knew of in the UK, which happens to be in Bath. I asked them if I could do a show and in the true spirit of Xmas, they agreed and were happy to help.

The date for my performance of *X is for Xmas Market* was set for the 6th of December. On the 4th of December, the weather forecast for the week was looking pretty dire. Heavy rain was expected throughout the entire week, which wasn't really a surprise considering it was England in December.

If I decided to do my show in the rain, my props would get wet. This would be incredibly dangerous because the wet props could slip out of my hands and would likely hit someone in the face – probably an old lady or a small child (again!). I don't know about you, but I really didn't want to hit an old lady or a small child with my props; therefore, I had to find another solution. Also, I don't like getting wet. I'm not sure what I was thinking by planning an outdoor show at this time of year. The likelihood that it would be raining, even before I had checked the forecast, was already statistically very high.

This left me in a bit of a pickle. I had to find an alternative venue beginning with 'X' and I needed to find one quickly. I knew that I had to do "Xmas-something" because options for 'X' were already very limited and we only had a few weeks left of "Xmas-ness". Then I thought, why not just Xmas? Xmas is such a large genre in itself that I could do an entire Xmas-themed show. I am aware that Xmas isn't really a location, in that I can't really do a show at, in or on it. But I was getting desperate and I'd already opened quite a few doors on my advent calendar, so *X is for Xmas* it would have to be.

Previously in my showbiz career, I had a dreadful experience performing a Xmas show that left me scarred for life. To be honest, the very thought of doing a Xmas show was dredging up all of these old feelings. To clarify, when I say showbiz career, I mean secondary school. And when I say Xmas show, I actually mean school assembly. Throughout most of my school life, starting in Year 6 at the age of ten, I would occasionally perform a juggling stint in my school assembly. The teachers encouraged and/or tolerated it, but either way, it was great for building up my confidence for performing. I was a kid performing juggling in a school assembly. It's fair to say that I was a cool cat. At least that's what I thought.

In my final year of school, I was aged fifteen and thought I'd perform a Xmas juggling routine. I dressed up as Father Christmas and hid in the sound and lighting booth that was situated at the top of a ladder, above the performance space. I sat and hid up there for the duration of the assembly until it was my moment to make a grand entrance.

My Head of Year introduced me as a special Christmas visitor, no doubt provoking a litany of rolled eyes, at which point I came climbing down the ladder holding my sack full of juggling props, and started my routine.

Foolishly, I had never practised juggling in the costume, so my first juggle as Saint Nick was in front of my entire school year. My trousers were too big, my hat fell in front of my eyes, my fake beard rose up and juggling club handles snagged on my baggy sleeves. An utter fiasco. It was bad. It was awfully bad. It was fifty shades of bad.

At the end of the spectacle that I had made of myself, I curmudgeonly packed up my props into my sack and desantafied myself. As the assembly was at the start of the day, and it had happened in front of my entire school year, I was fully expecting to be ridiculed by everyone that I saw.

Instead, what followed was worse. Nobody mentioned it. Nobody said anything about it at all. Not even

that it was bad. Not even that it had happened. It was so bad that it felt like the entire year group had unanimously agreed to never mention the atrocity again. I think I would've preferred the ridicule.

Even though it was many years after my festive school debacle, I knew that I had to overcome this ridiculous fear – and what better way to do that than to get back onto the metaphorical reindeer-saddle and do a Xmas show? I now just needed somewhere to perform, somewhere indoors and I needed to get it booked before the 23rd of December, as I had plans to visit my family for Xmas. It was the 4th of December, and as most places already had their Xmas entertainment organised months in advance, it was a challenging task. I needed help. I needed the help of a problem solver. I needed a **MEGA DUDE**. I called upon **CAMERON MD**.

In true **MEGA DUDE** fashion, Cameron didn't hesitate in helping me out. Within a day, he had arranged a place for me to perform *X is for Xmas* in the shopping centre and we had a date set. This man wastes no time. Why would he? He's a **MEGA DUDE**. In fact, from his flawless actions in so promptly saving our turkey and organising *X is for Xmas* – at such late notice – this might actually make him a **HYPER MEGA DUDE**. Before my eyes, **CAMERON MD** had evolved like a Pokémon into **CAMERON HMD**.

Somehow, I was now due to perform my Xmas show in five days' time – a Christmas miracle. I'd been so focused on getting a venue booked that I'd failed to realise that I didn't have a Xmas show. It was time to start creating. I knew that an easy fix would be to slap on a Santa suit and perform a juggling routine to Xmas music.

As with my previous traumatic experience, the Santa suit didn't really fit me and was hanging off my boney, slender frame. I guess it was designed for a more ample-bodied chap. Desperately not wanting to

repeat the disaster of December 2004, I needed to adjust the outfit. Luckily, my friend Angie Mack is a wiz when it comes to altering costumes and rapidly taught me how to tailor my festive wear so that it wasn't flapping all over my joints.

With three days until the show, I had a well-fitted costume but only had two short routines set to music. While my Santa suit had too much material, my show needed more. I spent the next few days experimenting with Xmas trees, decorations and wrapping paper. The joys of being self-employed.

For the show itself I was joined once again by Anton and, new to The ABC Tour team, John Godbolt: a fellow performer and friend that had access to a fancy camera and was willing to help out. John was filming the front angle of the show and Anton was on duty to film from unusual locations, such as from balconies and escalators.

The great thing about performing in the Galleries Shopping Centre was that I was on the ground floor but people could watch the show from a birds-eye view from both the first and second floor balconies. As I was dressed in true festive get-up, I told Anton and John that Xmas wear was compulsory. They did not disappoint and turned up as a lovely pair of elves.

Photos: The Void

With the show underway, people soon started to gather. Not many, but some, and some was all I needed. In total, *X is for Xmas* was a 20-minute show composed of all-new material. As well as the two new pieces performed to Xmas music, I had some other moments that I was very proud of. One such routine was with cigar boxes that I wrapped up to make look like presents. It involved balances, manipulations, tricks and ended with a volunteer catching the presents in a Santa sack.

For my big finale, I balanced a Xmas tree on my head, donned safety goggles, and got audience members to decorate the tree with silly-string as I rotated like a kebab spit. Prior to this routine, I gave the smallest kid in the audience a star, so that once the tree was lathered in colourful tinned tinsel, I would kneel down, still with the tree balanced on my head, and the child's parent would lift them up to put the star on top of the tree. In theory, this is a lovely, heart-warming ending to a Xmas show. In reality, it was a damp squib. I could never get down low enough for the child to put the star

on the tree. I needed a smaller tree, a taller child or for the ground to be further away.

After the show, we went for pizza. As we arrived to do the show in our Xmas attire, we didn't have a change of clothes, so it's fair to say that Father Christmas and his two elves stood out like sore thumbs.

We didn't let it faze us. Not only had the shows gone well, but I had also created a Xmas show that I'll be able to dig out of the loft each festive season to perform if I so wish. Most importantly, I had redeemed myself from my Xmas disaster of 2004. My Xmas show curse was finally lifted.

Y IS FOR YACHT

Yikes! I'd reached the penultimate show on the tour and no one was more surprised than me. There were many moments where I'd wanted to pull the plug, or felt like I'd never get to the end. Yet here I was with only two shows left. The light at the end of the tunnel was becoming noticeably incandescent.

Since *X is for Xmas*, I had taken an enforced break from the tour as I'd travelled to the other side of the world to perform at the Adelaide Fringe Festival. By the time I'd finished working and holidaying in Australia, it was now the beginning of April, which meant that the tour had taken a four-month hiatus. In a way, this was extremely helpful, as it meant that I could take a few months to focus on choosing the correct venues for the final two shows and book them up in advance, so that the tour could get going again as soon as I returned to old Blighty.

'Y' was always going to be Yacht. I love being at sea, I love yachts, and to be honest, I couldn't think of anything for 'Y' that would even come close to being as enjoyable as performing on a yacht. You may be surprised to read that despite a career spent doing juggling and comedy, I was still yet to purchase my first   yacht. With that in mind, my primary task would be to find one.

In order to know exactly

what I was looking for, I needed to know what made a yacht a yacht, rather than just a mid-to-large-sized boat. The dictionary definition states that a yacht is "a sail or power vessel used for pleasure, cruising or racing". Does that mean that a cruise ship and a sailing boat are both types of yachts?! I still don't know, but the good news was that the definition was vague enough that it meant that I had more than a few options if it became tricky to pin down a venue. The best-case scenario would be to find an old fashioned sailing ship with towering masts and vast sails that billowed in the wind.

My first lead was my friend Sally, who makes a living building and renovating boats. She was the only person I knew who was even remotely involved in that world, so I thought she'd have a good idea as to what my next step would be.

Sally didn't disappoint: she supplied me with the contact details for a charity called Sailing Tectona. Tectona is a large, stunning yacht with huge boastful sails (she wouldn't look out of place in any of the Pirates of the Caribbean movies).

In her 90 years, she had been used to ferry supplies, then as a chartered yacht, and now for training sailors – particularly for young people suffering from mental health issues or addiction. She was an absolute stunner, and I'm embarrassed to say that she seemed way out of my league – but it would have been foolish to not at least get in touch and find out.

Remarkably, after a swift phone call and a couple of emails, a course had been set for *Y is for Yacht*. They actually agreed to it; I couldn't believe my luck! I had an upcoming show aboard the hottest yacht in town, the performance would benefit a charitable cause and we had access to the yacht for a full day. They were well and truly on board with the idea.

My shipmates for *Y is for Yacht* were Luke (from the *U is for Underground* team) and Dan. With the car packed, we hit the road to embark on our journey from Bristol to Plymouth. The sun was shining and even though I knew nothing about sailing, it felt like the conditions were probably perfect for it.

As well as the classic car banter-bat being passed around, we spent a lot of the journey not really believing our luck. We were driving to sunny Plymouth to go on a stunning yacht for the day and perform out at sea. It felt too good to be true. Similar to that feeling you have when you first start a relationship with someone and everything is too perfect. So perfect in fact that it feels like something bad is going to happen any second to ruin it all, like finding out they are a Flat Earther, don't believe in vaccines, or they prefer their peanut butter smooth instead of the far superior, crunchy variety. But with Tectona, it didn't seem like there was a catch at all. We were giddy kippers.

We arrived at the harbour and made our way down the jetty, past the majestic flotilla until we saw her: Tectona. Her masts looming high over the surrounding boats, with the same smugness that the Burj Khalifa must have over its measly competitors for the "World's Tallest Building" trophy. Beautiful but humble. As Luke and I approached Tectona, Dan was ahead, filming us whilst walking backwards. We all agreed at that point that if Dan fell into the sea, saving the camera was our main priority.

The captain of Tectona, Aidan, and his crew gave us a warm welcome as we boarded. After a brief tour of the yacht, we sat down around a table in the galley with a cup of tea to discuss the day's plan. As our ABC Tour trio were new to the crew, Aidan had the idea of playing some simple group name games before our meeting began. This was great as it really made us outsiders feel like part of the team. Once the game was wrapped up, Aidan asked me what the plan was for the day and, all of a sudden, all eyes turned on me.

In all honesty, I hadn't thought this far ahead. I had an amazing opportunity to perform on a stunning yacht at sea, and I hadn't even stopped to consider how this was going to happen. I already felt privileged to have blagged my way this far into such an awesome situation but I didn't know what was supposed to happen next. I confessed my lack of forethought to Aidan, because I had never been on a yacht like this before, let alone being able to plan the day for one.

Aidan, unruffled, asked me "Ideally, how do you want this day to go?". Ideally, I wanted all three of us inexperienced baboons to be involved in the various bits and bobbins of sailing the yacht, such as pulling up the sails and driving it. Then we could head out to sea a bit, whack on the brakes and anchor her up so that I could do a show for the crew. After this, we could sail near some land, park up again, and get some members of the public onto the yacht for another show. Then, some more sailing, before heading back happy as Larry. If I was really pushing it, I'd like to make an ABC Tour flag for the ship.

I thought this was a lot to ask, especially the flag. Aidan replied with "Perfect. We'll get some lunch prepared for you too. Let's go. I'll get some material for the flag". *WHAT?!* Not only did he say that we could go ahead with my plan, but also they were going to give us lunch AND flag material. In ABC Tour history, this kind of positivity from venues was so unheard of – CAMERON HMD aside – that I was left slack-jawed.

The smell of the spuds boiling, mixed in with the gentle sea breeze was divine – it smelt like one of those fancy packets of salt and vinegar crisps. As the crew were prepping the sailing stuff, I was on all fours out on the deck painting The ABC Tour flag. I was with friends, who were helping me on an absurd project that had taken a lot of work to get to this point – and I really couldn't have been happier.

It didn't take long for the gentle wind to dry the flag, so we attached it to the rope and hoisted it up. Seeing the flag flapping in the wind gave me a sense of pride in all I'd achieved on the tour, despite the trials and tribulations I'd faced.

By this point, it was time to head out to sea and the crew of Tectona made sure that Luke, Dan and I were involved in the whole process. We were pulling, winding, steering, heave-ing and ho-ing wherever it was necessary. They really made us feel like we were part of the team, even if we were, in all honesty, probably slowing them down. Once the billowing sails were up, the yacht picked up the pace and it was time for me to nip down to the galley to switch personas from Jonboy, the fairly useless shipmate, to Jon Udry, juggler and comedian.

With the anchor dropped and the yacht bobbing gently in the waves, it was time to rock the boat. It felt incredibly odd to be spiffed up on a yacht, about to perform for a crew that had sailed out all this way specifically for me to do a show. I felt fortunate beyond belief.

I was aware that I had never had the chance to fully experience what it would be like to perform on a rocking, moving surface. When I perform on cruise ships, they are so large that it takes a rough sea to be able to feel the movement. With the yacht being a lot smaller, the mildest waves made her wibble.

Trying to steady myself on the constantly moving surface was unsettling. Yes, I had performed on a trampoline, but this was a different kind of challenging surface to stand on. A trampoline was consistent in its movements and, as such, was a lot more predictable.

On the deck of a yacht, out at sea, there were an entirely different set of issues. The inconsistency of the waves made the rocking of the deck very difficult to manoeuvre. This, chucked in with the breeze, made even basic tricks a lot more onerous.

If you are juggling and the floor moves – even by a little bit – when you throw your prop, it's not going to land exactly where you intended it to, because when the prop is airborne, you move

Photos: Luke Bailey

underneath it. I found that if I focused only on the yacht, and tried to block out my vision from everything that was beyond it, this really helped. If I looked at the skyline bobbing up and down, or up at the clouds passing the tip of the mast, this really messed up my focus.

I needed to "Be one with the yacht", something which, if Mr Miyagi was in this situation, I imagine he'd say. I found that if I kept my knees bent and focused only on the juggling, and not throwing too high, I could get through the show reasonably stress-free.

However, if I tried any tricks that involved looking up, the whole situation became a real issue for me. Juggling five clubs, no problem. Bouncing a ball on my head, impossible. This is down to the fact that, out of the corner of my eye, I could see the clouds in the sky rocking from side to side. A distraction that I could not, in this circumstance, avoid.

The show for the crew went surprisingly hitch-free. Post-show, we were treated to a spot of lunch and before we knew it, our relaxing break had come to an end. It was time to haul the anchor up and head on to our next location. Our captain, Aidan, had the idea of heading to my homeland, the Cornish coast, before anchoring up once more to see if we could entice some members of the general public onto the yacht for an impromptu show. With the sails hugging the breeze, we were off again on the next leg of our adventure.

Approaching the famously stunning Cornish coast, we dropped the anchor for the final time, as the water was too shallow for Tectona to park up snug to the coastline. Along with the skipper, Dan and I took the tender dinghy to shore to try and rustle up an audience. This proved to be remarkably easy because, let's face it, who wouldn't want a free opportunity to board Tectona to see a juggling show? Certainly easier than getting someone into a white van at a retail park.

Tectona is a big beauty, but one of the issues we faced was that she could only hold a maximum of fifteen people, not because there wasn't space for more, but because she is coded by the Maritime and Coastguard Agency (MCA) for up to 15 people, so that is her legal limit. This meant that we had to temporarily ditch some of the crew so that the audience could come on board to watch the show. With only the tender dinghy to get people on and off of the yacht, this turned out to be a bit of a 'fox, hen and bag of grain' situation. After a lot of to-ing and fro-ing, the yacht reached full capacity and our audience of landlubbers settled in for the show.

The second show was a lot easier as we were close to the land, so I didn't have to fight with the breeze and the waves. It kind of felt like a normal show to be honest – just on a yacht. It was perfect for me, as I was fairly exhausted from the ship work that we had been involved in: pulling up the anchor, hoisting the sails, steering the yacht etc. Not only did it make me use muscles that barely get used, but I think I even discovered a few new ones.

With a successful second show completed and the audience returned to port, I was exhausted but with a big old smile glued to my face. The sail back to Plymouth was peaceful and it felt like a great time to reflect on not just how perfect the day had been, but how far I had come on the tour to be able to get to this point. Looking up at The ABC Tour flag still flapping away in the wind, I felt chuffed to bits. The day could not have been any more perfect and this was largely down to the beautiful Tectona and its incredible crew. I'll be forever grateful to them for that.

Z IS FOR ZOO

Z oos have held a magical place in my heart for as long as I can remember. Ever since my childhood days of meticulously lining up toy plastic animals around the house, I have been obsessed with all forms of wildlife. I would spend hours doing this and get so engrossed and swept up in my imagination that I actually thought I was a zookeeper.

When I was four and finally old enough to go to nursery school, I remember telling the teachers that I had a pet elephant and a giraffe at home. I remember knowing that this wasn't true but I was also convinced that I wasn't exactly lying. I really did believe that I had an elephant and giraffe at home. Each day when I would arrive at the nursery, the teachers would ask about my elephant and giraffe and I would state, matter-of-factly, that they were doing just fine and that I had needed to feed them that very morning.

A year or so later, I thought it was about time I started my own zoo. After all, I was almost six years old and it was time to start getting real. Perhaps I thought I should start my own zoo because I was riddled with the guilt that came from telling people I had a zoo when I clearly didn't.

Like all businesses, I started small. I rinsed out a used ice cream tub and carefully placed some foliage inside, before introducing my zoo's first attraction into their new habitat: ants. I'd collected a few of the crawling critters from an ant's nest I found in the garden and added them into their new enclosure before then sealing the tub with the lid. I wouldn't want them to escape! After all, no one likes to go to a zoo to see nothing but empty enclosures.

My second attraction was a worm. This slimy little fella lived in a jam jar that was full of

mud. Clearly, it was only a matter
of time before people were going to
be queueing up around the block to
see my exotic animals, so I needed to
be fully prepared with the good stuff.

My final attraction to the zoo was
a frog that I permanently borrowed
from my neighbour's pond. The frog
lived in an old fish tank that we had sitting
around the garden. His enclosure was really something special. He had a section
for sitting on land and a section for swimming, with all of the trimmings. By
trimmings, I really do mean trimmings from hedges and trees. The zoo was
ready.

The night before the zoo's grand opening, my brother mentioned that I really
shouldn't keep the lids on the jar or the ice cream tub or else the animals would
suffocate. To prevent this, I took the lid off of the jar, knowing that the worm
wouldn't be able to get out. As for the ants? I'm no fool. I didn't take the lid off.
Instead, I took a pen and stabbed away at the lid to make a dozen or so holes
to ventilate the tub. When I awoke, the ants were mysteriously gone. Sadly, this
meant that I had to shut the zoo down before it even had the chance to open.

Having been fixated on animals my entire life, and despite the animal-related
issues I'd experienced previously on the tour, it was obvious that I had to do *Z is
for Zoo* as my grand finale. This was not only because there are not many other
good options for 'Z' but also because it's a chance to go to the zoo – and I'll
take any opportunity I can get.

As I started my search to find a zoo, the main issue I found was that they
often had a place for performers to do shows; however, it was rarely near
animals. I was adamant that I wanted it to look like a zoo from wherever I
was performing. Either I wanted animals in the background or, in the best-

case scenario, I would be in with the animals. I knew that the latter would be unlikely.

The majority of the zoos I contacted were surprisingly interested in me performing The ABC Tour for them, but we kept running into the specific performing space issue. Then I remembered a conversation I'd had with a juggler, Hazel, who goes to my local juggling club, about her parents owning a small zoo up near the Lake District. She kindly put me in touch with her parents and Jack Williams, who was the manager at Lakeland Wildlife Oasis.

They were very keen on me performing at their zoo and, as they seemed to have a strong personal bond with the animals, were happy to be a little bit more lenient with regards to me performing in the enclosures with them. On top of this, they were also celebrating Hazel's Dad's 70th birthday at the zoo and wanted my visit to coincide with the party.

This was music to my ears because it meant I wouldn't have to drum up an audience in the Lake District for the last show, as there would already be people there for the party. *Z is for Zoo* was well and truly on.

For the four and a half hour journey north, I was joined once again by Will and Dan. I was filled with a giddy excitement: partly because I was anticipating an exciting day ahead but also because I was about to reach the end of an incredibly long journey – and I didn't mean the car ride. Today was the finale of a project that had taken two years to complete, or three years if you include the year it had taken before just to get it going. It was a big day and I was feeling particularly thrilled to finally see The ABC Tour through to its conclusion.

On arrival, we were greeted by Hazel's mum, Jo Marsden. Jo gave us a tour of the zoo, explaining to us which enclosures I was allowed to try and do a show in and which were off-limits. I was incredibly surprised by how comfortable she was with regards to me being in the enclosures. But this was her zoo – and her animals – and she seemed to know all of them and their individual personalities exceptionally well.

After our brief tour, Will, Dan and I had lunch and planned our day around the enclosures that we were permitted to turn into temporary venues. As I was allowed to perform in a number of places in the zoo, we decided that it would be good to do a number of small shows for both the humans and the animals. One of the reasons I did The ABC Tour in the first place, was to try and bring my show to people that wouldn't normally get the chance to see

Photos: Will Huddy

it, by performing in unusual places. Today was my final attempt at trying to entertain animals on the tour, by bringing the show directly to them in their own enclosures.

Suit on and food in my belly, I was ready to perform in my first venue and meet my first mammalian audience of the day. Furry, with dexterous hands, opposable thumbs, trademark striped tail and the cutest face around, but enough about Dan. All the way from Madagascar: the lemurs.

This enclosure housed two types of lemur, the ring-tailed and the red-fronted – both would be tough competition in a cuteness contest. Jo had suggested that I perform with the lemurs first as it coincided with their feeding time, which meant that I could get in the enclosure and feed them as part of my show. This was quite possibly one of my all-time favourite show perks.

As I started setting up my equipment around the furry fellows, not only was I a visitor to the zoo but it was apparent that I was also a visitor in the lemurs' home. I was anxious as to how they would react to the show, and really didn't want to upset or agitate them in any way. Jo assured me that they were used to all sorts of noise, as their enclosure was situated at the edge of the zoo and was right next to a busy road. During my setup, I put some music on to see how they would react. True to Jo's word, they were completely unruffled.

With a small group of people ready to watch the lemur-feeding-juggling-show, and the hungry lemurs wondering why there was a smartly dressed man holding a microphone in their house, it was time to start. I was sandwiched between a goggling audience in front of me and the curious lemurs lurking behind me. I had been in the lemur house for quite some time now and up until that point, they had been unperturbed by my presence.

For my first routine, I decided that I would do a ring juggling routine to music so that I could determine how the lemurs would react to both the music and the juggling: a sort of gauging two lemurs with one stone strategy. I started the show and, fortunately, the music seemed to have no effect on them other than curiosity. The lemurs drew closer to me as if they knew that soon I'd be the one feeding them tasty, fruity snacks.

The very moment the juggling ring parted from its grip in my hand and soared centimetres into the air, the lemurs vanished into a puff of fur and split to the safest depths of the enclosure.

Initially, I assumed it was the erratic movement of the props, but then I tried the same thing with juggling balls and they didn't seem threatened at all. In fact, they actually seemed to enjoy it. I performed the ball juggling to individual lemurs that were adorably perched politely on branches, with their large inquisitive eyes doing their utmost to follow the balls in the patterns.

It turned out they did like juggling, but just weren't fans of rings. Jo suggested that it could be that the rings may have resembled a net, and that could've brought back bad memories of being captured. Who knows? Maybe they just thought that ring juggling was a bit naff.

Our next stop in the zoo was the smallest enclosure of the day and of the tour: the Swinhoe's striped squirrels. The enclosure was so small that for an audience to watch, they couldn't be any larger than about four, which was lucky. I wanted to use this enclosure to try and perform my teacup and teabag routine as, once I was in there, there wasn't much room to do anything else.

The striped squirrels were no larger than the size of my hand and zoomed around at an alarmingly energetic pace, constantly bouncing off the walls and darting from branch to branch as if they had been fed something that they shouldn't have. Their hearts beating quicker than a Buddy Rich drum solo: one second they were there, the next they were on the other side of the cage, almost as if they had been teleported.

Once I entered the enclosure and positioned myself ready for the "show", I could barely move. It was like being in a telephone box but with lower ceilings and full of squirrels that were off their nuts.

I had to be very careful about how I moved so that I wouldn't squish one of the little critters. Saying that, they were so quick that I doubt I would be able to squish one even if I tried. I didn't try. After the few minutes it took to perform my teacup routine in the cage, I was out of there. Looking back at the footage of this moment, it didn't come out great. The squirrels moved so fast that you could barely see them, so it just looked like a suited man in a cage drinking tea.

My final afternoon show took us to the meerkat enclosure. I love meerkats. They are like cats and dogs and rats rolled into one – constantly on the lookout for food, parties or mischief. Most likely food. Jo said that I could go into the enclosure and do some juggling but I was not allowed to touch them, which is a shame because I absolutely wanted to steal several. I juggled clubs over them whilst they clambered and clawed at my ankles, perhaps requesting better tricks,

or that I do it with fire (I still hate it when people request that). Most likely, they wanted me to feed them or scram out of their house.

I felt more nervous about juggling over the meerkats than I did about juggling over the pigs in *P is for Pig Pen*. Perhaps this is because when I visualised dropping a club on a pig, it wouldn't do much harm. But a club to a meerkat would do some serious damage. It was a mistake to say this out loud to Jo as she watched through her fingers and firmly said, "Don't club my meerkats". It's that kind of advice that got me through the show. Don't club a meerkat. Simples.

Animal performances completed, we had a few hours to kill until the evening show. Jo showed us the location where she thought the show would work best. It was a modestly sized room that enclosed a plethora of vivariums holding a variety of exotic snakes, spiders and lizards. I had no problem with this as they were enclosed. What I did have a problem with were the gigantic, hairy, nasty-looking fruit bats that were free-roaming and hanging from the ceiling. Bats.

My worst nightmare. Bloodsucking (probably) bat-stards the size of my thigh, erratically swooping across the room that I was due to be performing in in a few hours time. The way that they squeaked and hissed sounded malicious. No one else heard them hiss but they definitely did. My final show of the day and the entire tour, was in a bloody bat enclosure full of snakes, lizards and spiders. Brill.

The audience of approximately forty party guests arrived and settled down for the show. They didn't seem fussed at all about the bats. Perhaps this was because they were either vampires or not wimps.

It was lovely to have a proper audience (no disrespect to the lemurs) for the last show of the tour. For the majority of the performance, I have to be honest and say that I always had one eye on a bat; despite this, whenever they swooped towards me, I couldn't help but flinch. It felt like, at moments, they were trying to sabotage my show. Classic bat behaviour. At the end of the day, I should give them a break. Up until this point, bats had never done anything bad. But this was in pre-Covid-19 days, so now the jury is out on them.

Despite the bats, the show was very enjoyable to do. It was lovely to perform to such an enthusiastic crowd. To be fair, even if the show had went incredibly badly, I probably wouldn't have noticed as I was so ecstatic that the tour was done. Finally, it was over. I enjoyed it but man, what a silly idea it had been. It was a privilege to finish the tour at such a lovely venue surrounded by such curious animals of all shapes and sizes, as well as the lemurs, squirrels, reptiles and meerkats.

EPILOGUE

When I was 15 years old, I was experiencing the most stressful time of my life so far: my GCSEs, the final exams in secondary school. Good GCSE results promise to mould your future into an idyllic and prosperous dream. Of course they are stressful, as they should be. One bad day in an exam hall could lead to a future of slinging bin bags into a truck whilst the bin juice marks its territory on your uniform. There was immense pressure to cram more and more information into our brains by the day. Like any container, I felt like my head could only contain so much. I couldn't help but think that every time I learned some new information, another nugget of knowledge would be evicted from my skull.

I wasn't good at school, but I wasn't too bad either. I coasted somewhere in the middle. I excelled at certain subjects such as Maths, Science and Music, but couldn't get my head around English. Maths and Science appealed to me because I like puzzles and the questions tended to have a definitive answer.

In English, I used to dread the moment where the class would be reading a book together and we'd all have to take turns to read a page out loud. Whenever it was my turn, my palms would get sweaty and I'd stutter and stammer over words. Reading out loud still freaks me out now at the age of 32 – and I talk on stage for a living.

I also didn't get along with English, because I couldn't write, spell, construct sentences or comprehend grammar very well. I mean, I could do it but it was always a struggle. Even now, when I am writing by hand, I often write the letters of a word in a different order. *Wait, am I dyslexic? What a time to find out! At the end of a book?!* Ben (the editor of this book (he'll decide whether we can have brackets (within brackets)) will be the first to tell you how much I've learned about grammar and spellling whilst writing this book.

As part of my English GCSE, I had to hand in a creative writing project. This had to be a story that I had made up, and had a certain word count: I can't remember exactly how much but it was more than 1,000 and less than 2 billion. I kept putting off the writing because, you know, homework is boring and juggling is fun. It got to the night before I was due to hand in my story and I hadn't even started. I was freaking out. And then I had a genius thought; Why don't I copy a story, which would be the type of story that I would have probably written if I had time, and then call it my own?

They should have awarded extra bonus gold GCSEs for this smart boy! I dug out an old juggling book called The Encyclopaedia of Ball Juggling by Charlie Dancey and remembered that there was a story in the back called *Zen and the*

Perfect Juggler. I thought, *There is no way the teachers would know that I copied this*. It was niche enough that no one in school would ever have read it, and it was about juggling so surely they'd think I must've written it. I then spent the next few hours typing it up. It took ages, but to be fair, it would've taken a lot longer to actually create a story.

The next day, with bags under my eyes, I handed in the story. A few days passed and I was well and truly relaxed in the thought that I had actually gotten away with it. I was in my music class when Mrs Griffiths, the Head of English, burst in and demanded to speak to me outside. She asked me very matter of factly if I had genuinely written *Zen and the Perfect Juggler*. Thinking that she was impressed by my work, I lied through my teeth and said yes. She asked me again, probably because she was amazed that I could produce such a high standard piece, and was preparing herself to shower me with praise. I humbly said yes, again. Her face turned puce and she looked like she was sucking on a lemon. And then she snapped. The rage burst out of her as she verbally laid the smack down on me.

It turned out that she suspected plagiarism, so she typed the first few lines of my homework into Google and up had popped the entire story. She thought I had lazily copied and pasted the whole thing. Aiming to dig myself out of the trench, I told her that I didn't do that, and I'd in fact typed it all up from a book. Surprisingly, I didn't redeem myself, and if anything, I think I fanned the flames. "This is unacceptable! A writer doesn't steal stories and call them their own. You're not a writer!". The yelling continued as she completely tore me a new one. As well as giving me two weeks in detention, she also said that she was contemplating taking away all of my GCSEs. I'd leave school with nothing. Being a bin man wouldn't be so bad. Actually, hanging on to the side of the truck looked quite fun to be honest.

It turned out that even Mrs Griffiths had a heart and she didn't take away my chances of a happy future. I was allowed to keep my GCSEs, which – to this day – I have never needed.

Considering my academic background, I am amazed that I have written this book. If you have gotten this far, then you have to admit to yourself that it doesn't completely suck either. I'm pretty chuffed with it, to be honest. Not only have I written a book without copying it from someone else (See! I can do it, Mrs Griffiths!), but it's about a subject that I am very proud of.

Even now, a few years on, The ABC Tour has been the most challenging and time consuming project that I've ever worked on. It was 944 days from the first meeting with The Void about setting up the Kickstarter, to the end of *Z is for*

Zoo. In a pessimistic nutshell, it took 944 days to plan and complete a twenty-six date tour. This averages out as one show every thirty-six days.

Across these 26 shows, I performed for humans, fish, pigs, squirrels and lemurs. I was snubbed by dog shelters, ice rinks, monkeys and roller skaters. I was covered in ants and bitten by a pig, had sprained my ankle and had snow fall into my bum crack. I'd been too hot and too cold. I'd done shows while bouncing, rolling and sailing. I'd had audiences that were naked, knitting and watching online (not at the same time, that I know of).

These are just some of the memorable experiences that I will take away from The ABC Tour. I had some of the best and worst shows of my life during it but I am grateful for every single one of them. Would I do it again? Absolutely not. Well, that's not strictly true. If each show were paid and someone other than me was in charge of organising it, then I'd consider it! But repeating it in the way that I did? No way.

My one regret with this book is that I wanted to try and sneak in an alphabetical paragraph; each word beginning with the next letter of the alphabet. I'm sure that a good writer would be able to do this, but here is my attempt…

"A book can do everything; from going higher if juggled. Knowledge lets my noggin's operational performance quiver. Really should try using vest wipes (e)xternally, you zoo-keeper."

Not only does it not make sense, but there's no way I could put that nonsense into a book. See? I told you at the start, I'm not really a writer. Maybe Mrs Griffiths was right!

During the process of writing this book I have learnt a lot about grammar and storytelling, but I never really got the hang of endings

ACKNOWLEDGEMENTS

A tour like this wouldn't be possible without the many people that have helped along the way. I have done my best to acknowledge everybody involved but if I have forgotten you, I am very sorry. Feel free to add your name to this list with your writing implement of choice. To indicate which shows people helped out at, I have put a capital letter after their name, like a badge of honour or a degree. For the shows that people attended for the fun of it, whilst off the "ABC Tour Clock", I have put a lower case letter (excluding *I is for Internet* because I had no way of knowing exactly who was watching).

Firstly, the twenty-six venues that facilitated The ABC Tour and their staff:

Hannah (A) at Bristol Aquarium, **Gary** (Bt) and **Alex** (Bt) at The Bristol Loaf, **Tom Humphreys** (C) at Usk Castle, **Gary Shrimpton** (D) at Door World, **The Eden Project**, **Jennifer Davis** (F) who worked at Stonebury Learning Forest School (she is now an author and has a great book about forestry, which you can find on this website www.wanderwondergrow.com), **Sophie and Nigel** at Hours Space Gallery, **Sam Young** (H) at Shotgun Barbers, **Tina Backhouse** at The Island Jail Cells, **Kate Evans** (K) at Immediate Media, **Bristol Central Library**, **Sarah Hanson** (M) at Wild Futures Monkey Sanctuary, **David Piper** (N) at Spielplatz Naturist Club, **Adam Woodhouse** (O) at the British Origami Society, **Valerie Bickford-Beers** (P) at Pennywell Farm, **The Canteen Quiz Night**, **Dorset Sk8 Jam**, **Snozone**, **Doug McColm** (T) at Freedog, **Gerry Cottle** at Wookey Hole Caves, the venues for *V is for Van* (**Circomedia** and **Times for Tots Nursery**), **Cameron HMD** (WX) at The Galleries, **Aidan Begbie** (Y) at Sailing Tectona, and the **Marsden family** (Z) at Lakeland Wildlife Oasis.

Thank you all so much for allowing me to do my juggling and comedy nonsense in your venues. This tour wouldn't have happened without you.

As well as venues, many people helped out throughout the tour that I have to give a huge thank you to. In no particular order:

The Void (bX) - Filmed, edited and brainstormed many ideas to get the Kickstarter live.

Sam Veale (AB) - Filmed and helped out at *A is for Aquarium* and *B is for Bakery*. He also wrote the foreword for this book, helped proofread it and has always been there to help brainstorm ideas.

Anton Mackman (FgHIJKLNOQRSTUV) - Designed posters from B-C, E-Z. Edited most of the videos for the online series. Allowed us to do I is for Internet in his house. Drove the vanue. Generally helped out on 14 of the shows.

Loz James (V) - Organised for me to perform *V is for Van* at the nursery.

Marky Jay (QV) - Loaned me fire clubs, gave helpful advice about performing to children (which I didn't apply), and organised for me to take over his quiz for a week for *Q is for Quiz*.

Dan Edwards (IKLMNPQRSUVYZ) - Took photos at *K is for Knitting Club*, sneakily filmed like a crafty camera chameleon for twelve shows, boosted morale by remaining naked at *N is for Naturist Resort*.

Courtney Prokopas (ILMNOPQ) - Booked L-P, edited H-Q for the online series, brainstormed ideas, wrote the questions for *Q is for Quiz*, took photos at L-P, generally helped out.

Angie Mack (dIg) - Altered my Santa suit so that it wasn't too baggy. Let us use her house for *I is for Internet*.

Lynda Musgrove (x) - Taught me to ice skate for the ice skating show that never happened.

Laura Curry (K) - Yarn-bombed the mic stand for *K is for Knitting Club*.

Jugglers of the British Juggling Convention - Made me loads of origami to take to *O is for Origami Convention*. Generally just being awesome.

Auntie Rick - Taught me how to roller skate so that I could wow the attendees at *R is for Roller Disco*.

Emily Dixon - For the inspiration that she says she gave me.

Nat Whittingham - Taught me how to trampoline and not break myself in the process.

Luke Bailey (UY) - Took photos and generally helped out for *U is for Underground* and *Y is for Yacht*.

Will Huddy - Helped set up, film and take photos at *W is for Window* and took photos and generally helped out at *Z is for Zoo*.

John Godbolt - Filmed *X is for Xmas* whilst dressed as a lovely elf.
This book wouldn't have been possible without my editor/designer/grammar
teacher **Ben McCabe** (i) and the marvellous **Thom Wall** from Modern
Vaudeville Press for publishing it.

Finally, I have to thank my delightful proofreaders **Owen Reynolds, Sam
Veale, Molly Whitehouse, Fiona Wightman**, and **Anton Mackman**. Yew have
maid shure their arr, , know spellin miss Takes or airers with punktuation in; in
this book. Thank you.

Whether you helped a little bit or a lot, I appreciate you all so much for
everything that you did. Having you on board made this tour that little bit less
stressful. Thank you.

As well as the book, we've got it all on video:

THE ABC TOUR
DOCUMENTARY

Scan the QR code or go to
jonudry.com/abctour
to find out more.

ALSO PUBLISHED BY MODERN VAUDEVILLE PRESS

Juggling: Or How to Become a Juggler (annotated edition)

Rupert Ingalese, annotated by Thom Wall
ISBN – 978-1733971201
99 pages
MSRP: $15 USD

The fully annotated edition of Rupert Ingalese's 1921 "how to juggle" manual. This book covers basic juggling technique, tricks with hats and canes, practice methodology, and more. Ingalese's manuscript provides an interesting look at the state of juggling pedagogy in Britain's music hall era. Annotations by juggler and circus researcher Thom Wall bring insight and context to Ingalese's descriptions and instructions.

Pottery in Motion

Sam Veale
ISBN – 978-1733971232
71 pages
MSRP: $15 USD

British juggler Sam Veale's *Pottery in Motion* is the first of its kind - a straightforward book that provides aspiring plate spinners both the specifics of the props (such as plates, sticks, and rack) and comprehensive instruction on the skill of plate spinning itself. This small but detail-packed guide appeals to individuals looking to learn plate spinning and provides the knowledge to take it to a performance-ready level, just add practice.

Juggling: From Antiquity to the Middle Ages

Thom Wall
ISBN – 978-0578410845
129 pages
MSRP: $25 USD

As with dance, so with juggling—the moment that the performer finishes the routine, their act ceases to exist beyond the memory of the audience. There is no permanent record of what transpired, so studying the ancient roots of juggling is fraught with difficulty. Using the records that do exist, juggling appears to have emerged around the world in cultures independent of one another in the ancient past. Paintings in Egypt from 2000 BCE show jugglers engaged in performance. Stories from the island nation of Tonga place juggling's creation with their goddess of the underworld—a figure who has guarded a cave since time immemorial. Juggling games and rituals are pervasive in isolated Inuit cultures in northern Canada and Greenland. Though the earliest representation of juggling is 4,000 years old, the practice is surely much older—in the same way that humans were doubtlessly singing and dancing long before the first bone flute was created.

This book is an attempt to catalogue this tangible history of juggling in human culture. It is the story of juggling, represented in art and writing from around the world, across time. Although much has been written about modern jugglers–specific performers, their props, and their routines–little has been said about those who first developed the craft. As juggling enters a golden age in the internet era, *Juggling: From Antiquity to the Middle Ages* offers a look into the past—to the origins of our art form.

Spanish Edition:

Malabares - desde la Antigüedad hasta la Edad Media: la historia olvidada de lanzar y cachar

Thom Wall, et. al.
ISBN – 978-1733971263
179 pages
MSRP: $25 USD

Malabares - desde Antigüedad hasta la Edad Media, es un divertido viaje por países, por épocas. Desde el Antiguo Egipto y sus ya famosas malabaristas profesionales de la tumba nº 15 de Beni Hasan, a los juegos para niñas de la isla de Tonga y otras zonas del Pacífico Sur; pasando por los edictos del rey Alfonso X de Castilla sobre la regulación de los juglares o los antipodistas aztecas actuando ante el Papa Clemente VII en el siglo XVI. También reserva un espacio al final del libro para, aprovechando su faceta de lingüista, realizar unas reflexiones acerca de la propia definición de la palabra "juggling"[malabarismo] a lo largo del tiempo y sus orígenes. Es, por tanto, un libro ideal no solo para malabaristas o cirqueros, sino para cualquiera con curiosidad sobre la historia, en especial de aquellos hechos que en ocasiones pasan más desapercibidos en los textos cotidianos.

A través de este libro aprendemos sobre leyendas y juegos antiguos, fantaseamos con grandes artistas y actuaciones que nunca podremos ver y que nos hacen dudar sobre esa tan manida sentencia que a veces afirma "esto nunca se ha hecho antes". -*Malabares en su Tinta*

Juggling: What It Is and How to Do It

Thom Wall, et. al.
ISBN – 978-1-7339712-5-6
224 pages
MSRP: $25 USD

Juggling: What It Is and How to Do It teaches learners of all ages how to juggle – one of the world's oldest artforms. With a kind demeanor, humor, and enthusiasm, this authoritative manual explains the process of juggling through four different modalities, bolstered by the latest physical education research. *Juggling* is an accessible primer that a middle-schooler can hit the ground running with, or that families can enjoy together. The result of six years of work by 2021 International Jugglers' Association *Excellence in Education* award winner and former Cirque du Soleil juggler Thom Wall and featuring guest chapters by some of today's juggling masters, *Juggling* provides a wealth of content for even the most serious adult learner.

Book plus Juggling Kit!
Includes juggling balls by Alchemy Juggling

MSRP: $60 USD

This exclusive kit makes the perfect gift for any aspiring juggler. Includes one copy of *Juggling: What It Is and How to Do It* and three professional-grade beanbags.
Beanbag specs: 90g ea., approx. 2.75" diameter.
Machine washable / dryable. Made in USA.

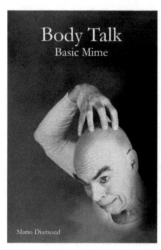

Body Talk: Basic Mime

Mario Diamond
ISBN – 978-1733971218
73 pages
MSRP: $15 USD

Body Talk: Basic Mime covers the fundamental skills of mime in an easily accessible workbook format. Diamond brings over 40 years of teaching and performance experience to *Body Talk*, which includes rich photography illustrating various mime techniques.

"[*Body Talk: Basic Mime*] should be required reading for any theater participant looking to incorporate elements of mime into their routines." - *Midwest Book Review*

Artistes of Colour

Steve Ward, PhD
ISBN – 978-1-7339712-7-0
317 pages
MSRP: $25 USD

In a society that places an increasing value in ethnic diversity and cultural identity, the contribution that performers from a variety of ethnic backgrounds made to the development of the circus in the nineteenth century is often dismissed and largely forgotten. Using contemporary records and images, *Artistes of Colour* explores the wealth and depth of talented black and other performers of colour, and the contribution they made to the success of the nineteenth century circus. Ward draws iconic figures from the margins of history and gives them the recognition they deserve, illustrating what the BBC calls "a field of study that has been overlooked far too long."

Circus Games

Compiled by Lucy Little & the American Youth
Circus Organization (AYCO)
ISBN – 9781733971225
124 pages
MSRP: $15 USD

With over 100 games organized for optimal use in
cooperative movement based settings, this is a must
have for every circus school, teaching artist, and arts
education program! Games are organized by age,
number of participants, energy level, and social/emotional learning outcome,
and also includes special notes for working with a variety of populations that
may require adaptation or modifications to each game. Find more info about
the project here: https://www.americancircuseducators.org/gamesproject/

Circus Training Journal

Thom Wall & Rebecca Starr,
Consultant editor: Sarah Baker
ISBN – 978-1-7339712-9-4
9×6" paperback
380 pages
MSRP: $20 USD

What's measured is managed! The *Circus Training
Journal* is the result of a year of collaboration
between Thom Wall and Rebecca Starr, head aerial
coach at Circadium: School of Contemporary
Circus. This undated journal, which spans three months of daily training, tracks
workouts, nutrition, goal-setting, and more. Heavyweight groundwood paper
optimized for ballpoint and pencil.

Mongolian Contortion:
An Ethnographic Inquiry
(monograph)

Mariam Ala-Rashi
Monograph / no ISBN
100 pages
MSRP: $10 USD (eBook)
$15 USD (archival print)

This project introduces the performance art form of Mongolian contortion by examining its theories and functions before and after the establishment of the Mongolian State Circus in 1941. Through qualitative research it investigates events that led to the transformation and re-emergence of Traditional Mongolian Contortion in Mongolia as an international export to the West in recent years. Mongolian Contortion examines the numerous challenges contortionists face with traditional aesthetics and presentations, and proposes solutions for the safeguarding of this art form.

China's Bending Bodies:
Contortionists and Politics in China
Mariam Ala-Rashi

Chinese Contortion (monograph)

Mariam Ala-Rashi
Monograph / no ISBN
138 pages
MSRP: $10 USD (eBook)
       $15 USD (archival print)

This research study proposes an introduction to the performance art form *contortionism* by examining its theories and functions throughout the 20th and 21st century. It considers themes including the appropriation of contortionism during the golden age of Hollywood and discusses definition issues between contortionism and other disciplines that highlight body flexibility, such as gymnastics and yoga. By examining the genesis of contortionism in ancient China, it aims to explore parallels between the origins of Chinese contortionism and the establishment of Chinese acrobatics. It later dissects the political use of contortionism in socialist China and the development and institutionalization of acrobatic troupes since the founding of the People's Republic of China in 1949. Drawing upon a Foucauldian perspective, it further examines the parallels between the Western training of soldiers during the 17th and 18th century, and methods of traditional Chinese acrobatic training in the 21st century at the *Beijing International Art School*. This monograph includes data from a wide range of literature, material evidence, oral history, current media reports, and considers recent work in anthropology, archaeology, and political history. It, therefore, offers the interested reader, the scholar, the contortionist and contortion practitioner a substantial treatise about the art-form *contortionism*.

COMING SOON

Circus Games (v1.1)

Compiled by Lucy Little & the American Youth Circus Organization (AYCO)
MSRP: $15 USD

Due to the huge success of the first edition of *Games for Circus Educators, Organizers and Innovators*, the American Circus Educators (ACE) are creating a 2nd edition. This book is comprised entirely of games submitted by ACE community members across the country!
This book contains the original 100+ games from the first edition, as well as new games, variations on, and expansions upon games in the first edition. Conditioning games, aerial games, and games for preschool-age children are now included! Play on!

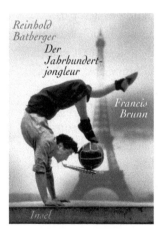

The Century's Juggler

Reinhold Batburger, translated by Kathrin Wagner, edited by Thom Wall
MSRP: $25 USD

He throws a ball in the air and makes millions. And millions of people watch – and did for more than fifty years.
His performance takes seven minutes, and that's his life. Reinhold Batberger tells a family story – the story of a world career, the story of the life and art of juggler Francis Brunn (1922-2004).

Opulence & Ostentation

Paris. — *Le Cirque d'Hiver*

Steve Ward, PhD
ISBN: TBD
MSRP: $25 USD

Mention the word circus and often the first thought is of the Big-Top. But before the advent of this iconic structure, early 'circus' performances were given in the open air. Later came temporary wooden structures and then canvas tents. During the nineteenth century, particularly the latter part, a wave of civic building saw many grand permanent circus venues built across Europe, and beyond. A few of these buildings still exist today as circus venues; others have been repurposed, and many have long since disappeared. *Opulence & Ostentation* traces the fascinating and colourful history of the permanent circus building.